Chenal de St Vincent
Chaptte St Vincent
ou de Trompeloup
la Guippevill
Frenea
le Ro Signot
la Pitar de
la Dinde

les Portes
le Juge
la Pte Metairie
les Plaines
les Plaines
la Romefort
les Gadelles
les ptes Gadel
la montagne Ecluse
le Pa

la Monconseil
la St Aulaire
la Beaumone
la Bezelini
la Manche
la Forgette
le Bois
le Chapitre
L'Trep
laGra
la

Pouialet
Padarnac
Caubet
Cagnon
de Casteja

Chenal du bahet
Mn de Pauillac
Patras
Isle de Patras

Pauillac
la Capette
le Bisconac
Praduna
Bages
le Pais
Cordeillan
Tastins
Mn de Pellegrue

la Salle
le Frène
la Gde de la Motte
la Merlesse
les Minimes
Qua

St Lambert
dit St Mambert
le Prat
Fonbadet
Balogues
le Bo
la Tour
la Badane

Parc Neus
Baril
Parc de Jamon
Chante Allouette
Parc de Miot
la Longée
la Crou
Puyladeuil
Touffaut
Cap de Haut
la

Parc de Pinon
Vouteton
Morne
l'Hopital
d'Hotel
de Ville
St A

la Pastouralle
les Ardouins
la Pouyade
Menaut
le Coude
la Palu
d'Almoi

les Garbeuac
St Julien
de Reginac
Port
Talabot
le Long
Langon
le Tastu
Bavolier
le Pré du Roy
la P.

le Brenu
le Camp
la Salle
Esp
Deseroia
la Valade
Caillet
Gd Jean

la Fon du Long
la Mouline
la Justice
L'Oeil Negre
Chepas
Maucailleau
Hortevie
Beychevelle
la Font bouleau
de l'Hopital
le Port de
Beychevelle
Ste Gemme
Lannessans

Segonzac du
la Brousse
les Tourneaux
les Brios
Tirut
la Grange
de la
Cur de Haut
Saugeton

Pauillac

The Wines and Estates of a Renowned Bordeaux Commune

Pauillac

The Wines and Estates of a Renowned Bordeaux Commune

Text by STEPHEN BROOK

Photography by MICHAEL BUSSELLE

Foreword by JANCIS ROBINSON

MITCHELL BEAZLEY

Pauillac
by Stephen Brook

First published in Great Britain in 1998 by Mitchell Beazley,
an imprint of Reed Consumer Books Limited, Michelin House,
81 Fulham Road, London SW3 6RB and Auckland

A CIP catalogue record for this book is available from the British Library

ISBN 1 85732 352 1

The publishers will be grateful for any information which will assist them in keeping future editions up to date.
Although all reasonable care has been taken in the preparation of this book, neither the publishers
nor authors can accept any liability for any consequences arising from the use
thereof, or the information contained herein

Created, edited, and designed by Norfleet Press Inc, New York, NY

Editorial director: John G Tucker
Designer: Abby Goldstein
Copy editor: Patricia A Wyatt

The text for this book was composed in Dante, a typeface originally designed by
Giovanni Mardersteig and Charles Martin in 1952. It was redesigned in 1991 by Ron Carpenter.
The display type was set in Cochin, a typeface designed in 1977 by Matthew Carter.

Color separations by Bright Arts Ltd in China
Printed and bound by Toppan Printing Company in China

ENDLEAVES: *Detail of Bordeaux from the Carte de France de Cassini (1744-1767), courtesy of the Map Division of the New York Public Library*
FRONTISPIECE: *The entrance to the cellars of Château Lafite-Rothschild*

Contents

Contents

The Other Wines of Pauillac 149

CHÂTEAUX

La Bécasse · Béhèré · Bellegrave · Bernadotte · Cave Coopérative: La Rose Pauillac
Colombier-Monpelou · Cordeillan-Bages · La Couronne · La Fleur Milon · La Fleur Peyrabon · Fonbadet
Gaudin · Haut-Bages-Monpelou · Haut-Linage · Pibran · Plantey · Saint Mambert · La Tourette · La Tour Pibran

The fermentation vats, Château Pontet-Canet

The vineyards of Pauillac in autumn

Foreword

Like most places that have lent their name to wine, Pauillac evokes many different responses, depending on the context, even to someone well into their third decade of writing about wine.

I will always associate Pauillac with my first stay there in the early 1980s. The heavy, aqueous atmosphere of the Médoc and its villages in summer was at its most obvious. Pauillac, much more a business than a tourist centre, is heavily influenced by the grey Gironde from which it is separated by a bleak promenade. (Saint-Julien, Saint Estèphe and Margaux are all set back from the estuary that connects Bordeaux to the Atlantic.) I was then researching my own book and had to spend the night after a sumptuous dinner at Château Lafite in what was at that time Pauillac's only available tourist accommodation, the then dilapidated Hôtel France et Angleterre, its cordial name belied by decades of neglect. Our makeshift room, apparently carved out of several awkward spaces, conformed to no geometrical form I have ever encountered. Its lone attraction, that it overlooked the promenade, dissipated the minute Pauillac's motorcyclists began to use it as a racetrack in the small hours, coinciding with the height of the mosquitoes' assault on our tender English flesh.

This whole sorry experience was to be fully exorcised when I next stayed at the France et Angleterre in the mid 1990s, by now fully reconstructed and run with efficiency and warmth. I spent a week there with a film crew and a thoroughly awkward amount of paraphernalia. Pauillac turned out to be one of the most agreeable billets we encountered during our many months touring the world of wine.

As a wine taster, on the other hand, I view Pauillac with nothing but enthusiasm. Not just because such a high proportion of its wines are excellent and a quite extraordinary proportion of them superlative, but also because the characteristics of a typical Pauillac are so delightfully marked: deep, deep colour combined with a remarkable combination of concentrated mineral and fruit flavours, and appetising tannins, together with a level of alcohol that seems designed to inspire rather than inebriate. There are not many beacons in the rugged terrain the blind taster is expected to traverse but Pauillac, bless it, is one of them.

And then of course as a wine lover (which is rather different from a wine taster) I, like countless others, put Pauillac on a pedestal – a very special pedestal for consistently offering me the chance to experience red wine at its most subtle, most digestible, most long-lived and, more often than seems geographically justified, most refined.

Even the most determined Francophobe has to admit that Bordeaux in general and Pauillac in particular are the guiding lights for producers of red wine all over the globe. No other patch of land has succeeded in yielding so much magic in bottles that can be kept for decades, sometimes centuries, continuing to evolve and improve. Balance of all the elements that go into making up great wine is the key to this success. A quite disproportionate number of the greatest wines I have encountered have been produced in the apparently undistinguished vineyards surrounding this rather ordinary-looking small town north of Bordeaux (all of which Michael Busselle's magic camera has captured in their most heart-stoppingly beautiful aspect).

A book devoted specifically to Pauillac is long overdue, and Stephen Brook is an admirably reliable guide. One of relatively few professional writers with a long history of drinking serious wine in general and red Bordeaux in particular, Stephen has approached Pauillac as conscientiously as he has the full range of subjects on which he has written books: from Israel to opera, or perhaps more relevantly, from Sauternes to the South of France.

As one would expect from such an experienced journalist and sound judge of wine, this is no romanticised monograph, no promotional sales pitch. It is a genuinely useful and thoroughly up-to-date wine-drinker's guide to this most glorious of Bordeaux communes. When criticism is due, he does not hesitate to mete it out, whether it be of town, wines, proprietors, or sales techniques. He pulls no punches in his assessments of individual bottlings or management philosophy.

On the other hand, he is delightfully unswayed by popular opinion and official rankings, studiously pointing out as only an informed insider could, which châteaux are producing wines of a quality, and therefore value, above their commonly held station.

It would not be too difficult for any competent hack to put together a collection of essays on the most famous wines of Pauillac – those included in the 1855 classification. The sign of really serious footslog on Stephen Brook's part is his useful and detailed assessments of the less well-known properties, the so-called petits châteaux of Pauillac. This is not as easy as it may appear, for several of them have headquarters more closely resembling a shed rather than a grand country house, and a shed well hidden in a backstreet at that. Our guide relentlessly managed to track down virtually every one, and taste its wines.

One particularly valuable feature of this book is its topicality. Most of the research was conducted in 1996, so we are able to benefit from up-to-date assessments of such hot topics as that vintage's wines, the use of concentrating techniques in the cellar, inflation in the market-place, journalists in the tasting room, AXA's inexorable invasion, and even that apparently contradictory innovation, the Médoc marathon.

In short, this book is the first genuinely user-friendly guide to the epicentre of the world of fine red wine.

– Jancis Robinson

Garden statuary, town of Pauillac

A tree-lined road in Pauillac

Introduction

❧

'Pauillac.' It's not the easiest of names to pronounce, and perhaps it doesn't linger as easily in the mind as the evocations of 'Margaux' or 'Pomerol'. Every drinker of good Bordeaux wines knows the wines of Pauillac, but more likely under their exalted château names. Nor is everybody who enjoys and admires Lafite or Mouton or Lynch-Bages necessarily aware of the commune from which they come.

Terroir is crucial in Bordeaux, as in every great wine region of Europe, but it is perhaps less obviously important than in, say, Burgundy or Champagne. In more northerly regions such as those where grapes have to struggle to ripen fully, every nuance of soil and microclimate counts. A twist of exposure here, a band of red porphyry there, a crisp wind coursing down a valley – all these can have a profound effect on the wines.

The same is true in Bordeaux, but because it is a sunnier, more southerly region, the precise differences between one part of a vineyard and another can be less marked. Bordeaux, and certainly the Médoc, that triangle of land perched like a dunce's hat over the great port, boasts perhaps the finest soils anywhere on which to grow red grapes.

Much of the Médoc is composed of beds of gravel, deposited in turn over subsoils of marl or limestone or clay. This soil is sufficiently impoverished to ensure the vines must struggle to survive, but sufficiently rich in nutrients to ensure the wines are packed with flavour and nuance. The best sites are superbly drained. The Atlantic climate of Bordeaux usually ensures that the vines have enough annual rainfall to thrive, while the gravel soils help that water to filter down. There is nothing more calculated to damage a vine than soggy roots.

In the Médoc everything seems to come together in perfect harmony: grape varieties, soil, climate, ventilation, and exposure. It would be invidious to say that any one of the great communes of the Médoc – that string of villages that includes Margaux, Saint Julien, Pauillac, and Saint Estèphe – is superior to any other. There are those who adore the delicacy and elegance of Margaux at its finest; others find the finesse of a top Saint Julien totally seductive; yet others may prefer the power and opulence of Pauillac. Saint Estèphe has many admirers, myself included, but I don't think there are many who would argue that it produces their favourite wines out of the entire Médoc.

Pauillac, however, can easily claim to be the most renowned of all the communes of the Médoc simply because it contains no fewer than three first growths: Lafite-Rothschild, Latour, and Mouton-Rothschild. Scour the rest of the Médoc and, in the first-growth league, there

A fishing jetty along the Gironde estuary

is only Château Margaux. Although the 1855 classification, which established the hierarchy of growths, is inevitably out of date, I don't believe anyone would wish to dispute the supremacy of its choice of *premiers*. They were elected in 1855 because of their track record, and they remain supreme nearly 150 years later for exactly the same reason.

THE LIE OF THE LAND

The four great communes of the Médoc achieved their reputation because of their proximity to the Gironde. There is no doubt that this proximity to water has a profound effect on the microclimate. In Pauillac the vine growers will tell you that a great vineyard site is one from which you can see the water. And by and large that is true. The Médoc is flat. The highest point in Pauillac is a scant 30 metres. These high points are formed by gravel ridges known as *croupes*, and the very finest vineyards are located along the gentle slopes of these *croupes,* usually within viewing distance of the grey waters of the Gironde. Perhaps the primary benefit conferred by the estuary is protection from frost. In spring, frost can attack the vines, encasing the growing buds in a shell of ice, and as the sun rises the buds can roast to a black nubble.

In Pauillac the vineyards close to the water, notably those of Château Latour, are hardly ever frozen, whereas a mile or so inland the damage, as in 1991, can be overwhelming. Proximity to water also affects the ripening cycle, usually making the development of the vines more precocious. This can be of crucial importance. The precocity of Latour has allowed it to pick fully ripe grapes about a week earlier than more inland estates, and sometimes that week has made the difference between a perfect harvest and a rain-sodden one.

For all the differences between sites within Pauillac, what is striking about the region is its homogeneity: that expanse of gently sloping gravel *croupes* coated with vines. In 1996 there were 1,114 hectares of vines in production, producing some 62,300 hectolitres of wine, which represents an average yield of 56 hectolitres per hectare. The commune is subdivided by a number of streams, insignificant as water-courses, but important in providing drainage channels and natural barriers between varying *terroirs.* To the north, separating Lafite from Cos d'Estournel, is the Jalle du Breuil; to the south, separating Latour from Léoville-Las Cases, is the Jalle de Juillac. Another stream, the Chenal du Gaet, just south of Château Pibran, separates northern from southern Pauillac.

THE HISTORY OF PAUILLAC

For all the celebrity of the Médoc, and for all the occasional snootiness of the French as they look down their aristocratic noses at wines of the New World, this is a relatively new wine region. Many wine-producing zones in the south of France were sources of good wine in Roman times, and even earlier. The Graves, so close to the city of Bordeaux, was developed in medieval times. But the Médoc only became a significant wine-producing region in the seventeenth century. There would have been vineyards there in medieval times, though records are scant; such wines would have been primarily for local consumption. And despite a single reference to 'Pauliacus' in the works of the Roman wine-appreciator Ausonius, there is no evidence that this was a wine region in Roman times.

Today the Médoc presents itself to the visitor as a rather flat and drab region, devoid of picturesque landscape. It can hardly compete with the rolling hills of the Premières Côtes or Entre-Deux-Mers. Of course the noble châteaux and their parklands add variety and often charm to the region, but no one would claim that the Médoc is intrinsically beautiful. There are some charming spots in the far north of the region, where polyculture still prevails, but they are few and far between in the major wine-producing communes.

The Médoc presents a benign and tranquil image to the visitor, which would not have been the case before the seventeenth century. In medieval times the Médoc was a swamp, difficult to traverse; roads were inadequate and only the Gironde provided a reliable means of communication with Bordeaux and the rest of the world. Pauillac became a major port and supported an international maritime community that included English, Danish, Protestant Dutch, and Jewish Portuguese merchants. It enriched itself by requiring ships entering the estuary to hire pilots from Pauillac. The town also supported shipyards and cooperages.

In medieval times most of the land had been owned by *seigneuries,* such as those of Lafite and Latour, and by ecclesiastical institutions. Many properties would have been operated as farms, not primarily as vineyards, although small vineyards undoubtedly existed. By the seventeenth century many of these estates were in the hands of noble families and politically well-connected members, or even presidents, of the Bordeaux *parlement.* It was these men who developed the vineyards of the Médoc and made them prosperous. A map by De Belleyme, published about 1720, shows vineyards as mere patches among a landscape dominated by pine woods, briar patches, and rye fields. The map suggests a topographical battle between the *landes*, the sandy, marshy pine woods that stretch inland for miles along the southwest coast of France, and the partly cultivated fields and vineyards of the eastern side of the Médoc.

The discerning palates of the British, in particular, soon discovered the virtues of the wines of the Médoc. Leading growths such as Château Margaux and Château Haut-Brion in the Graves were firm favourites, but so were the wines of Pauillac, especially Lafite and Latour. Their high prices were surely a reflection of their quality, and all eighteenth and early nineteenth-century classifications were based on the prices the wines fetched. Then, as now,

The vineyards in winter

there would have been no exact correlation between price and quality, but over many decades wines can only sell at a premium if the market believes that high price is justified. That was certainly true of the wines now recognised as the first growths of the Médoc. Wines such as Lafite were ordered in substantial quantities by the British royal family and by statesmen such as Robert Walpole. By the 1730s their reputation was firmly established.

The long reign of Louis XV was a time of considerable prosperity for Pauillac. Bernard Ginestet, in his book *Pauillac*, reprints a classification based on prices drawn up in 1776. Lafite and Latour share top honours, Mouton is second class, Pichon third class, Pontet-Canet fourth, and the fifth class includes Lynch, Ducasse, d'Armailhac, and Milon; Croizet is consigned to seventh class.

By the end of the eighteenth century the Revolution partially destroyed the commercial structure that had been built up over the two preceding centuries. The châteaux did not market the wines themselves but shipped them in barrels, usually through brokers and other intermediaries, from the port of Pauillac. Nor were the wines bottled; château-bottling is a very

recent phenomenon. They were shipped out in the spring following the harvest and would have been stored or bottled at their destination.

With the Revolution many estates were sequestered and their proprietors arrested. Monsieur Pichard, the then owner of Lafite and a powerful figure, formerly in the Bordeaux *parlement*, lost his head to the guillotine. Others, such as Joseph de Pichon-Longueville, survived. The confiscated estates were usually put on the market by the state and sold off as a *bien national*. Many newcomers acquired the estates but they were not always able to maintain them. In those days bad harvests were more frequent than good ones, maladies of the vine were rife, and disappointed or bankrupt owners found themselves having to dispose of their estates just a few years after acquiring them. Moreover, tariff barriers impeded exports, diminishing the market. Some of the new owners were businessmen who had prospered in the post-revolutionary era; others were foreign merchants involved in the wine trade in Bordeaux.

By the middle of the nineteenth century a whole new category of owners began to take an interest in the vineyards of Bordeaux: the bankers of Paris. These were heady times in France when large fortunes

Garden flowers at Château Pichon-Longueville

were being made. The reign of Napoleon III brought prosperity to the nation and two decades of stability.

The Rothschilds were the most famous of the bankers, but they were by no means the only ones. The Pescators and Halphens had also started buying properties here in the 1840s. Although these rich Parisians may have enjoyed coming down to their Bordeaux estates from time to time, they were not bought primarily for recreational purposes. By this time wine was, as it had been before, an investment. After all, the quality of the region's wines had been proven over a period of some 150 years. The Médoc may have been a newcomer to wine production, but it had certainly made up for lost time. Its wines had long been sought after and fetched high prices.

Émile Castéja, the owner of Châteaux Batailley and Lynch-Moussas in Pauillac, comes from a Médocain family whose origins can be traced back many centuries. (On De Belleyme's map there is a hamlet marked near Pauillac named Castéja.) He is also a member of one of Bordeaux's most respected *négociant* families and is a jealous guardian of the historical traditions of the region. Despite his learning and a capacious library of books about wine, Castéja is no sentimentalist.

'Remember,' he told me, 'in the nineteenth century, wine in Pauillac was already an industry.' He is right. All the structures of the modern Bordeaux marketplace were already established: the intimate relationship between the château as producer and the *négociant* as sales force and distributor was long in place. Fortunes could be and were made from wine, as new investors were well aware.

❧

THE CLASSIFICATION OF 1855

The codification offered by the famous Classification of 1855 made an enormous difference. Little about it was novel, but it confirmed the assumptions that the wine trade and wine drinkers had been making for decades. There was considerable objection to the drawing up of an official classification, which was designed to accompany the presentation of French wines at the Great Exhibition of 1855 in Paris. Earlier classifications did not differ greatly from that of 1855, but the novelty was that the new hierarchy was devised by the *courtiers*, the local wine brokers, who had been tasting, buying, and shipping the wines for generations. They knew them intimately. The classification was not mere connoisseurship: it was based on the prices fetched by each growth, as good an indicator as any of the relative ranking of each property.

A cottage near the village of Artigues

Although the Classification of 1855 remains useful, it must be remembered that the wines of the mid-nineteenth century were likely to have been very different from those we taste today. It was not until the early years of the nineteenth century that the grapes we think of as classic Bordeaux varieties – Cabernet Sauvignon, Cabernet Franc, Malbec, Petit Verdot, and Merlot – were widely planted. It seems probable that by the mid-nineteenth century Cabernet Sauvignon was already the variety of choice in the Médoc. Merlot was a later arrival, becoming widely planted as recently as the 1850s. Other varieties, including Syrah, had a place in the vineyards too. Nor were the wines solely composed of the production of the vineyards from which they supposedly came. It was standard practice at the time to doctor the wines, especially in lesser vintages.

In the late 1980s, while dining at a small restaurant in the Corbières region of southern France, the owner told me how tank-loads of robust local wines made their way north to be blended with lacklustre Bordeaux. I don't know whether the story was true, but it certainly could have been part of a venerable tradition. Wines were said to be *Hermitagé*, that is, spiked with a good dose of strong red from the Rhône. There was nothing underhand about it; it was regarded as a form of judicious blending, and no doubt a dollop of ripe Syrah would have done wonders for an unblended barrel of unripe Cabernet from a wet vintage.

TRADITIONAL WINEMAKING

Vines were trellised differently in the nineteenth century and would have been trained up poles rather than splayed along wires. Émile Castéja recalls seeing small plots of vines trained up poles as recently as the 1970s in some artisanal vineyards in the southern portion of Médoc. Today the most widely used form of trellising is *Guyot double*, with two branches trained along wires, pruned to six or seven buds. The usual density of plantation is from 7,000 to 10,000 vines per hectare.

Winemaking, too, was a far cry from the highly analysed, intensely monitored techniques of the past few decades. Near the entrance to the *chais* at Château Batailley is a painting from about 1900 which shows the wine being made. The bunches were destemmed by hand (as they still are, partially, at Mouton) and then put into *treuils*, large wooden troughs, in which the grapes were broken up. The must was put into small containers and lifted up into wooden fermentation vats. Then the remaining grapes were added. There was no pumping at that time. The cap was broken up with a stick to which a kind of ball was attached.

Modern winemakers would be horrified by the insanitary conditions. It could take two or three days to fill a vat. There was no temperature control, so growers would resort to picking in the evenings to ensure that the grapes added to the vat were cool. After a relatively quick fermentation the vat was covered, and from a hole near the top, a pipe curved down into a bucket of water. This isolated the contents of the vat from the air and allowed a further maceration to take place without oxidation. (Jack Fardègue of the minute Château Haut-Linage still uses this method.) About four to six weeks later the vats were emptied and the wine poured into barrels, where it would remain for up to three years, with frequent rackings. Quite a lot of press wine would have been added.

An old *cuvier*, now a museum, can still be seen at Château Lynch-Bages. Here the grapes were destemmed through a slatted frame and fell into a shallow trough called a *conquet* in which the destemmers were standing, ready to crush the grapes by foot. The system resembles that of the stone troughs found in the Port region, where grapes are still foot-trodden at certain traditional estates. The *conquet* had a gutter at either side from which the must flowed into a wooden vat, and since the trough was on rails, the flow could be directed into any of the vats in the *cuvier*. Fermentation and maceration would then occur in the usual way.

When the *cuvaison* was judged to be complete, a worker would be told to jump into each vat with a bucket on a pulley to extract the grapes, which were then taken to be pressed. After pressing (in a hydraulic or a vertical press, some of which are still in use at a few properties, as everyone agrees that they give a fine quality of press wine), the remaining pulp, called the *marc*, would have been spun in a suspended metal tube called an *émietteur*. Its interior was lined with teeth, which helped macerate and aerate the *marc* so that it could be pressed for a second time. It seems clear that many nineteenth-century wines would have contained a high proportion of press wine.

Freshly harvested grapes

Cabernet Sauvignon clipped from the vine

The new harvest shortly before being crushed and destemmed

The ageing of the wine, or *élevage*, was in the hands of the *négociants*. Once the wine was made it was shipped in barrels to Bordeaux where the *négociants* raised the price of the wine according to the demands of their clients. The role of the château was simply to make the wine. For the last 30 years all châteaux have undertaken their own *élevage*, giving them greater control over the quality of the finished wine.

When tasting an old Pauillac there are many factors to bear in mind: the different vinification, the lower yields, the possible presence of obscure grape varieties in the blend, the strong possibility that wines from outside Bordeaux might have been added to give greater strength and body, the lottery of *élevage* – all would have led to a far less consistent product than we are accustomed to. I recall Pauillacs from the 1960s – such as the 1964 Château Pontet-Canet – which I first tasted in bottlings by English wine merchants. They were perfectly sound, but it was widely known that some merchants were more capable and reliable than others when it came to bottling wines drawn from cask.

The luxurious, prosperous times of the late nineteenth century came to a slow halt in the nation's wine regions when phylloxera struck. It took some years for its havoc to be complete, and many vines in Bordeaux survived until the early twentieth century. Eventually, the vineyards of the entire region were replanted on American rootstocks. Nor was phylloxera the

Cabernet Sauvignon approaching perfect ripeness

only enemy of the vine stalking the vineyards. Oidium was considered just as much of a threat, though its damaging effects were less permanent than those inflicted by the dreaded louse.

The early twentieth century was an unsettled time for Bordeaux in general and Pauillac in particular. Not only was World War I disruptive, but its political consequences had a profound effect on the fine wine market. The Russian market collapsed completely, many royal courts such as those of Prussia and Austria-Hungary vanished from the scene, and the Americans had the peculiar idea of imposing, or trying to impose, Prohibition. Things would get worse before they got better. The widespread economic depression and political crises of the late 1920s and 1930s also had a devastating effect on the market. Many celebrated *négociant* houses went out of business, and classified growths were declared bankrupt.

Many small estates disappeared as their owners sold off parcels in a struggle to survive until, in some cases, what was left was no longer economically viable. Vineyards vanished. Near Château Lynch-Moussas some vineyards were replaced by a pheasant farm and a hunting chalet; today the vines have been replanted. The meteorological climate was as dire as the economic. In the early 1930s there was a run of appalling vintages, during which some vineyards were ravaged by a form of mildew called black rot. The 1934 was an excellent

Merlot juice before transfer to oak barrels

vintage, but André Cazes, the former mayor of Pauillac and owner of Château Lynch-Bages, told me: 'In 1934, when châteaux ordered barrels from the local coopers, the coopers would take away one full *barrique* for every two empty ones they had delivered. Châteaux were simply giving away the wine.'

Then came World War II and the German occupation. Almost all the châteaux were taken over as barracks or officers' quarters, but the cellars were left untouched. *Weinführers* were appointed to ensure that soldiers and officers on an alcoholic binge did not take it upon themselves to organise vertical tastings from the leading châteaux. It was known that the thuggish *bon viveur* Hermann Goering had his eye on some of these cellars, but they survived the war without serious depredations by the Nazi high command. The *Weinführers* were often members of families of German origin who had become proprietors in the region; they thus held allegiance to both sides. Madame de Lenquesaing recalls how the antique furnishings of Pichon-Lalande were stored in a nearby barn and restored to the château after the German soldiers had retreated.

✌

THE MODERN ERA

After World War II there were some wonderful vintages and the market revived, but for most growers these remained difficult times. Then came the devastating frost of 1956, when icebergs were glimpsed down the Gironde, crushing small boats between them. The vineyards of entire communes were wiped out, which led to extensive replanting in the Médoc in the late 1950s and early 1960s. Vines need to be about 20 years old to give of their best, and so the increasing age of the vineyards of Pauillac as well as other communes have made a contribution to the outstanding vintages of the past two decades.

The region has weathered a series of crises since then – ghastly vintages such as 1972 – and commercial miscalculations, when mediocre wines were overpriced by growers and *négociants* cashing in on a gradually burgeoning market. Proprietors who weathered the storm are once again prospering. Newcomers are again buying estates that present owners are unwilling or unable to maintain. Some deplore the invasion of the Médoc by outside investors, but this is largely snobbery. Pauillac has always seen infusions of new blood and has been all the healthier for it. No one could have been more conscientious custodians of their *patrimoine* than the Rothschilds of Lafite and Mouton. In the 1950s and 1960s French-Algerians, the *pieds noirs*, arrived in large numbers in the Médoc. In the 1980s and 1990s it was Japanese companies, such as Suntory, and French insurance companies, notably AXA. The British have also been active proprietors. The first Rothschild owner of Mouton, Baron Nathaniel, was from the British branch of the family, and until quite recently the proprietors of Latour were the British company Allied-Lyons.

These large enterprises, with their seemingly limitless resources and a declared ambition to produce superlative wine, have been given the opportunity to buy some of the world's

Stainless-steel tanks, Château Lynch-Bages

A Pauillac vineyard in spring

greatest vineyards, in large part because of the draconian French inheritance laws. In 1981 inheritance taxes were doubled to 40 percent, and taxes are assessed on the value of the land. Nowadays a hectare of vineyards in Pauillac is worth between 1.2 and 1.4 million francs, making the owner of a medium-sized vineyard a multimillionaire, on paper. On the owner's death, the heirs might be required to pay millions of francs in taxes, which could never be generated by sales of the wines. In such sad cases – especially when the property is divided between numerous family members, some of whom may have no interest in wine and would rather realize their assets – the heirs have little choice but to put the estate on the market.

The arrival of large companies such as AXA will prove a mixed blessing. Their willingness to restore the once great but recently dilapidated Pichon-Longueville estate, and to construct architecturally innovative *chais,* is entirely welcome. On the other hand, AXA's purchasing power is so great that it can outbid most local growers when parcels of vineyard come on the market. Moreover, when a second growth such as Pichon-Longueville acquires a parcel of vines that formerly belonged to a *cru bourgeois*, it immediately has the right to use that crop in its *grand vin.* On the other hand, if a *cru bourgeois* acquires, usually by exchange, some vines that once belonged to a *cru classé,* the vines are immediately downgraded in terms of their *classement*. It is more likely that a second growth would use the crop from newly acquired vineyards in its second wine until it was quite certain of its quality and potential contribution to the *grand vin*, but it is under no legal obligation to do so.

Roland Fonteneau of the excellent little estate of La Bécasse tells me: 'I and other owners of smaller estates are grateful to the likes of AXA for helping to restore confidence in the region, but I also believe that in the long term they will ensure the disappearance of estates such as ours.' Another proprietor of Médocain stock pointed out that whereas the rich newcomers of the nineteenth century were families that took pride in their estates, the new investors in Pauillac are large companies rather than individuals, and companies never have the same attachment to a property that families do.

The watershed in Pauillac was the celebrated 1982 vintage. 'Before 1982,' says Michel Tesseron of Château Pontet-Canet, 'nobody talked about fruit in a wine. Ever since 1982 we have tried to pick when the grapes are mature. Before 1982 we were considerably less flexible and tended to pick the first grapes when they were still unripe and the last grapes when they were overripe.'

It is often remarked that there is no such thing as a bad vintage any longer in Bordeaux. That is patently untrue, though good wines, through luck or skill, can be made in even the least promising of vintages. However, it is undoubtedly true that the level of sophistication in matters viticultural and oenological is far higher than it used to be.

Various techniques are routinely employed to keep vineyard yields at sensible levels and to avoid dilution in the finished wine. Anti-rot treatments have become more efficacious, and when rot does occur, it tends to be less devastating than in the past. Malolactic fermentation, something of a mystery until it was unravelled a few decades ago by Bordeaux's most distinguished oenologist, Professor Émile Peynaud, is now far better understood. There are no more poorly maintained old barrels, and there has been a substantial investment in good-quality new oak, even among the most modest estates. There is a greater understanding of phenolic ripeness, ensuring that brutal tannins in wines largely devoid of fruit are a thing of the past. There are virtually no Pauillacs that I would describe today as rustic.

The differences between the wines of Pauillac derive from a number of factors: the *terroir*, which is more or less unalterable; the desire of the proprietor to make wines of high quality, which varies slightly; the introduction of greater selection and, consequently, of second wines; the blend of grapes in the vineyard, which is a mixture of tradition and choice; and the decisions that will establish the ratio of the quality of the wine to its price. Pauillac remains wonderfully blessed, especially in its *terroir*. As Jacques Babeau, the proprietor of La Fleur Peyrabon, remarked: 'If you can't make good wine in Pauillac, you ought to change your job.'

◆

GROWING THE VINES

Great wine, it is often said, is made in the vineyard. It is certainly true that without fruit of excellent quality no amount of wizardry in the winery can produce an outstanding wine. The *terroir* of Pauillac is predisposed to give richly flavoured wine, but that predisposition can be compromised if the vines are allowed to produce too much. The maximum yield is set at 60 hectolitres per hectare; some estates produce more than that from time to time, but in those circumstances they cannot declare their entire crop as Pauillac.

A cottage window in Pauillac

Despite the poverty of the gravelly soil, vines will thrive in a normal growing season if spared crop-reducing maladies such as *coulure* and if the sun shines brightly much of the time. During the planting booms of the 1960s and 1980s, certain clones and rootstocks were chosen that were simply too productive. The simplest way to control yields is to prune severely, thus limiting the number of bunches on the vine. But even strict pruning can't always deliver a suitably reduced crop if the vine is in its prime. Hence the common practice of green-harvesting, that is, snipping off bunches during the summer months. When the practice was introduced, it was viewed with horror by traditional *vignerons*, who were more accustomed to poor crops and couldn't understand why anyone would deliberately destroy up to a third of the crop.

Even today not everyone approves of green-harvesting. Pierre Peyronie of Château Fonbadet points out that, if you remove fruit, the vine will want to compensate. You may end up with fewer bunches, but those bunches are likely to be larger. Since the ideal is small berries with a low ratio of skin to juice, the production of unusually large berries or bunches is far from desirable. However, some growers who believe in green-harvesting say that if you remove bunches as late as possible in the growing season – that is, during the *veraison*, or period when the grapes change colour from green to purple – then you can both select the least ripe bunches for the massacre and give the vine the least possible time to compensate. Green-harvesting may not be a perfect solution to the limitation of yields, but it is surely better than nothing if pruning has not delivered the desired results.

In Pauillac it is legal to pick by machine. Very few of the major estates do so, but many smaller properties are enthusiastic advocates of the process. Certainly it is possible to pick with great speed with a machine, and to gather in a harvest before the threat of rain materialises. It is also true that harvesting machines are far more sophisticated than they were years ago and inflict far less damage to the vines. The argument against machine-harvesting is that no machine can be as selective as a human being – to which the enthusiasts for the machine reply that they would rather have a well-regulated machine than a band of indifferently trained student pickers with varying degrees of skill.

Whichever method is used, it is usual to scrutinize the grapes and eliminate bunches or parts of bunches that are either unripe or rotten. This process is called *triage* and takes place either in the vineyard or as soon as the grapes arrive at the winery. The advantage of *triage à la vigne* is that there is no danger of contamination, which can occur when rotten grapes are transported alongside healthy ones from vineyard to winery.

The vines in spring

However, the fact of *triage* is more important than the location. In the winery it can be more easily regulated, and many châteaux are equipped with a kind of conveyor belt along which the grapes travel on their way to the crusher/destemmer. Up to four sorters stand on either side of the belt and remove fruit that is not up to standard, thus ensuring that only ripe and healthy grapes end up in the fermentation vats.

MAKING THE WINE

These days all grapes are destemmed. The practice was introduced in the early twentieth century, and although there are other wine regions in France – such as Burgundy and Provence – where red grapes are macerated with their stalks, this is virtually unheard of in Bordeaux. A small proportion of the fruit is destemmed by hand at Mouton, but elsewhere machines perform the job with perfect efficiency. There have been times when stalks, which can add harsh tannins to the wine, have been retained. Michel Tesseron of Château Pontet-Canet recalls the very hot 1959 vintage, when the grapes were very low in acidity. In that instance, some of the stalks were retained, as that was the only method known at that time to add some acidity to the must.

The once inescapable problem that affected all winemakers working in troubled climates, and that includes Bordeaux, is that rain can wash out a vintage. Even if some of the crop is brought in before rain swells and dilutes the grapes and before moisture's ugly handmaiden,

Old fermentation vats, part of the museum at Château Lynch-Bages

rot, sets in, you may well have unripe grapes on your hands. Anyone who has tasted the green, vegetal 1972 Bordeaux will know what I mean. However, technology has come to the rescue, at least in vintages where the grapes are ripe but dampened or even swollen by unwelcome rain during the harvest. The traditional way to avoid dilution was to *saigner*, literally to bleed the fermentation vats. By siphoning off, say, 15 percent of the must, you end up with a higher ratio of skins to must, resulting inevitably in greater concentration. The drawback of this method is that you also lose sugar and aromatic potential.

Scientists have devised two machines to combat this problem. The first uses a technique called reverse osmosis, but its high cost has deterred Pauillac estates from buying these machines, though they are found elsewhere in the Médoc. Many estates have invested in a less expensive device which operates on the principle of *évaporation sous-vide*. Essentially it utilizes pressure to force evaporation without heating the must. With this method, up to 15 percent of the water is eliminated, leaving must that is far more concentrated. The beauty of the device, usually known as a *concentrateur*, is that it removes nothing but water. Since it concentrates all the elements in the must, any disagreeable elements will also be highlighted. Thus a potentially unbalanced wine may end up more unbalanced if the *concentrateur* is employed.

Oak barrels, Château Lynch-Moussas

Consequently, its primary use is to remove moisture in good vintages marred by rain, rather than to try to resurrect vintages that failed to ripen fully.

Many major châteaux have bought *concentrateurs*: Lafite, Grand-Puy-Lacoste, Pichon-Longueville, Pichon-Lalande, and Lynch-Bages. There seems to be no plausible objection to the technique as long as it is not abused (there is no evidence that it has been), and since the rules forbid chaptalization of must that has been concentrated in this manner, it can be argued that as a form of enhancing concentration, it is preferable to adding sacks of sugar to the fermentation vats.

One other technique is used at Château Croizet-Bages: heating the must to 55 degrees Centigrade right at the end of fermentation for a short period. Jean-Louis Camp, who instituted the policy, seems happy with the resulting extraction, but other winemakers in Pauillac, while not objecting explicitly to the technique, do worry that applying such heat to the must just might have damaging long-term consequences.

Everyone ferments the grapes at up to 30 degrees Centigrade, or a little higher towards the end of fermentation. Most large estates are equipped with temperature-controlled stainless-steel tanks, but there is a lingering affection for the old wooden vats that were the traditional

A regiment of tasting glasses

container some 30 years ago. Even cement is making a comeback at a few Pauillac estates, since, like wood, it retains heat efficiently and can give a smoother fermentation than the more capricious but more easily controlled stainless steel.

However, the nature of the container is not a matter of great importance. After the alcoholic fermentation, which takes about a week, the grapes are left to macerate for a further couple of weeks to extract further colour, fruit, and tannin. Over extraction is dangerous, so the length and temperature of the maceration are carefully monitored. The total period of fermentation and maceration is known as the *cuvaison*, which tends to be between three and four weeks. During the fermentation the must is pumped over (*remontage*), both to aerate the must and to moisten the cap (the floating skins near the top of the tank), but care has to be taken to ensure that *remontage* is sufficient but not excessive.

After the *cuvaison*, the wine is decanted off the skins, and the solid matter is pressed. Depending on the vintage and the quality of the fruit, a small quantity of the press wine may be blended back with the rest of the wine. Especially in weaker vintages, some press wine can add body and richness to the final blend.

The wine is then encouraged, often by heating the ambient temperature in the *cuvier*, to go through its secondary fermentation, the malolactic. This has the effect of lowering the acidity level of the wine, and is universally practiced. However there is a new trend for malolactic fermentation in barrels: the wine is poured into oak barrels once the press wine, if any, has been added. It's more complicated than malolactic in tanks, as the smaller volume of the barrels means that each one must be regularly monitored. The advantage, say its advocates, is that there is a better bonding between wine and oak, just as a white wine fermented in barrel is usually less starkly oaky than a tank-fermented wine that is merely aged in barrels. Decades ago the malolactic fermentation always took place in barrels, but there was no rush to complete it. If it was delayed until the spring, it didn't matter. These days there is pressure to get it over with as soon as possible to help the wine evolve rapidly. That means heating the *chais*, which can provoke bacterial infections.

Some winemakers freely admit that the primary purpose of malolactic fermentation in barrel is to allow the wine to take on a greater sheen of oak by the spring. March and April, following the harvest, is the time when the journalists and brokers descend on Bordeaux to taste the new wines. A great wine that is still closed up and dense may be less impressive in its youth than a lighter, fruitier wine with a lovely glaze of new oak. Since crucial commercial decisions are made at least a year before the wine has completed its barrel-ageing, or *élevage*, the first impression of the new wine can make a huge difference to its success in the market-place. I regret that competitive pressure within the wine trade and among wine journalists has led to definitive judgments being offered to the public at such an early stage in the young wine's evolution, but the process seems irreversible.

Another great change in Pauillac, as in other parts of Bordeaux, has been the introduction of selection. Certain châteaux, notably Lafite (with Carruades) and Latour (with Les Forts de Latour) have had second wines for decades, comprised of consigned lots made from young vines, as well as any satisfactory vats or barrels apparently not up to the standard expected of the *grand vin*. Over the last 10 or 15 years almost every château has followed suit. Usually between 35 and 60 percent of the entire crop is bottled as *grand vin* – it all depends on the quality of the vintage. Clearly, in great years such as 1990, a higher proportion of the wine was of sufficient quality to merit being bottled as *grand vin*.

Thus selection is a simple and effective way of increasing the quality of one's wine. Commercially it has the benefit of offering at a substantially lower price a wine that, by definition, is inferior to the *grand vin* but yet may have some of its style and quality. In outstanding years, even though the quantity of second wine may be reduced, its quality can often be superb. The one major château that for years refused to jump on this particular bandwagon was Mouton-Rothschild. Its reasons are discussed in the chapter on the first growths.

The Tour d'Aspic, built by the pious Mademoiselle Averous in veneration of the Virgin Mary

The *élevage* is a straightforward matter. The first growths use 100 percent new oak; other estates a lesser proportion. The notion that the more new oak the better is clearly a false one. (André Cazes recalls that, many decades ago, barrels were kept for up to 10 years or more at Lynch-Bages, and the use of new oak was minimal.) Latour, for instance, has the body and tannin and extract to support a lavish use of new oak; that might not be the case with a fifth growth or *cru bourgeois*.

The wine is racked every three months, and then a few months before bottling it is fined. Most châteaux fine with eggwhites, which are whisked and added to each barrel by hand; the eggwhite acts as a coagulating agent to which small particles or solids remaining in the wine adhere. The wine is then racked again to clarify it. Usually there is a light filtration before bottling, though a few estates eschew filtration altogether.

VISITING PAUILLAC

The most frustrating aspect of many visitors' tours of Pauillac is that it is difficult to actually buy the wine. Almost all the major châteaux sell their crop in the spring after the vintage to the various brokers and merchants located in Bordeaux. They agree on a price, and the brokers then sell the product worldwide. The château will offer its wine at an opening price, called the *prix de sortie*. Let's say this opening price is 100 French francs per bottle. A broker may then sell the wine (ex-duty and taxes) on to retailers and wholesalers in Britain or the United States or to restaurateurs for 135 francs. The retailers will list it to their clients at 160 francs. Everyone takes a profit (if the wine sells) and goes home happy.

Unfortunately, in years of speculation, a wine released at 100 francs may end up being acclaimed by a celebrated wine writer such as Robert Parker ('Parker 97' tells the customer all that he or she may want to know) and by the time it is listed by your friendly local wine merchant the price is 280 francs. Everyone makes money, but the château proprietor feels aggrieved, since he actually grew the grapes and made the wine, but some intermediary in Bordeaux has made far more money than he has. To alleviate this situation, château owners have begun releasing their wine in *tranches*. Thus 30 percent, say, of a potentially fine wine will be released at 100 francs. If it sells out within days, the château plays coy, and then releases another 30 percent a few months later, but this time offering the wine at 150 francs.

Since all the wine has been sold in advance of bottling to the Bordeaux *négociants*, there is no wine retained at the château for sale to visitors. There are a few exceptions. Many *crus bourgeois* make special arrangements enabling them to sell some of their production directly to private clients. Other estates, such as Pichon-Longueville, with links to their own *négociant* companies, sell directly to the public, though you may find the same wine cheaper at a local wine merchant (*caviste*) or supermarket. Pichon-Lalande also has a boutique where some older vintages are for sale. But these are exceptions. If you come to Pauillac with the primary objective of filling your car with a few cases of fine claret, you are likely to be disappointed.

Modern Pauillac is a rather sleepy town, its finest feature being the extended quayside. The nineteenth-century church has an immensely tall steeple that must have doubled as a lighthouse, guiding in ships from the estuary. There's a hotel of modest pretensions along the waterfront, and one or two even more modest restaurants. Given the considerable number of tourists that come here in the summer months, there is remarkably little provision for them, although a fine and very expensive Relais & Châteaux hotel and restaurant has been established at Château Cordeillan-Bages on the outskirts of town.

It's pleasant to stroll out onto the jetties and watch the boats bobbing in the Pauillac port, but there isn't much else to do. Continuing north up the coast in the direction of Saint Estèphe, you will pass the disused Shell refinery, a famous local eyesore, and then many small creeks in which fishing boats with distinctive butterfly-wing nets are moored. Out in the estuary they fish for eels, mullet, sea-perch, sole, and *piballes*. The latter are baby eels, little more than transparent squiggles with tiny black eyes. Time was when they would appear on local menus

The harbour at Pauillac

The town of Pauillac

for a few months, and be devoured with great gusto by the people of the Bordeaux region. In recent years the Japanese have discovered a taste for them, and they fetch such high prices (about 2,200 francs per kilo) that the local restaurants and fish merchants can no longer afford them. Other local specialties include pork tripe and *entrecôte*, which are grilled on *sarments*, pruned vine branches. You will look in vain for the famous *agneaux de Pauillac*, though I have spotted sheep grazing between rows of vines in the Charente region. The term now refers to a method of rearing lamb rather than to a region of origin.

Pauillac is not a particularly sociable place. Many proprietors are absentee landlords and live in Paris or elsewhere, even though they may take a keen personal interest in their estates and visit them regularly. Many other proprietors maintain their principal residence in Bordeaux, especially if they have children. As a consequence, many châteaux are little more than shells, used for receptions or to lodge guests during the high points of the wine calendar: Vinexpo in June, or the Union des Grands Crus tastings of the new vintage in March and April.

A meal at one of the châteaux can still be a formal occasion, when a visiting journalist or merchant is invited to meet some of the other proprietors. Formally attired waiters and waitresses will present a sequence of dishes; and an array of decanters, almost always filled with wines from the cellars of the estate, will trace the history of the domaine in liquid form. The Médocains certainly know how to entertain in style when the occasion demands it.

A relatively recent innovation has been the Marathon, which takes place each September and is attracting ever-increasing numbers. It begins on the quayside at Pauillac and the route winds for 42 kilometres through the vineyards, passing through Latour and down into Saint Julien. Initially some châteaux were rather dubious about the whole enterprise, but now everyone enters into the spirit of the occasion. At Château Mouton-Rothschild, the pebbles are cleared from the driveway in the interests of the soles of the runners' feet, and then replaced two days later. Most châteaux offer wine or other refreshments to the runners, who now come from all over France, and beyond. The Breton participants usually bring a cart filled with *brioches*, hauled by a team of runners and distributed to the bystanders. The night before the race one of the châteaux hosts a dinner for 1,500 people, usually held in tents in the grounds. This mixture of grandeur and informality has proved an enormous success.

The opening up of Pauillac to outsiders and visitors can only be a positive development. About 10 years ago a team of leading Bordeaux wine personalities invited a number of British journalists to lunch in London and urged us to criticize their approach. I pointed out that if you drove up Napa Valley you found dozens of invitations to taste and picnic and visit; drive up through the Médoc and all you see is imposing but closed gates leading to shuttered châteaux.

Since then, fortunately, there have been some changes. A number of Margaux properties welcome visitors, even during the sacrosanct French weekend. Progressive proprietors such as Jean-Michel Cazes fully acknowledge the importance of publicity, of familiarizing winelovers with his products and giving them a warm welcome should they have taken the trouble to make their way to Pauillac.

The visitors' reception centres at Pichon-Longueville and Pichon-Lalande are welcome developments: if visitors are shown the winemaking process without condescension, they will learn to better appreciate wine,

The Church of Saint Martin, built in 1827

especially wine of better quality, all the more. Not even Pauillac, for all its prestige, can rest on its laurels. I still find it irksome that, of the first growths, only Mouton has facilities for welcoming visitors. There is little to see at Latour, but for me it is the most awe-inspiring experience to stand in its vineyards or gaze at the ranks of barrels filled with, perhaps, the greatest red wine in the world. It cannot be too hard a task to show enthusiasts around, and as a marketing strategy, it should pay off handsomely in the long term.

Great wine is a combination of *terroir*, human skill, climate, sheer luck, and the personality of its maker. The sooner the proprietors of Pauillac assist winelovers to appreciate this the better.

A freshwater pond in Pauillac

Map of Pauillac

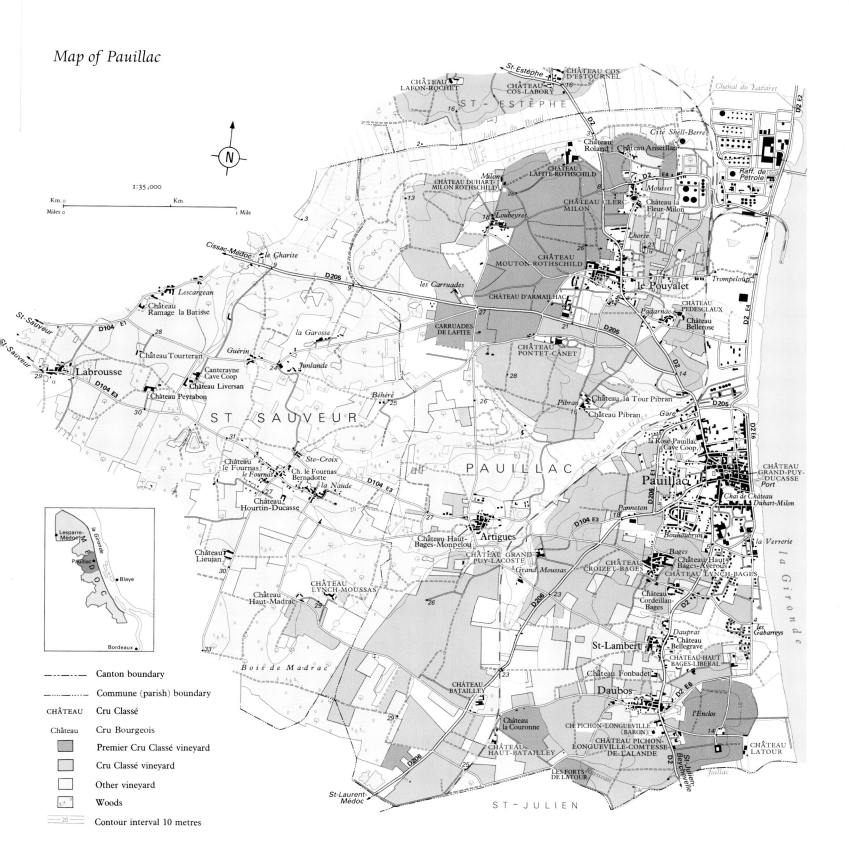

1:35,000

Km. 0 ————————— Km.
Miles 0 ————————————————— 1 Mile

Legend

—·—·—·— Canton boundary

—··—··—··— Commune (parish) boundary

CHÂTEAU — Cru Classé

Château — Cru Bourgeois

▓ Premier Cru Classé vineyard

▒ Cru Classé vineyard

□ Other vineyard

Woods

═20═ Contour interval 10 metres

The tasting room, Château Mouton-Rothschild

The First Growths

❦

CHÂTEAUX

Lafite-Rothschild • Latour • Mouton-Rothschild

Château Lafite-Rothschild

~

CHÂTEAU LAFITE-ROTHSCHILD

When the famous Classification of 1855 was released, it was Château Lafite that headed the list of the first growths. It is doubtful that anyone today would seek to produce a hierarchy within the hallowed ranks of the first growths. At this level of quality, preferences become a matter of personal taste. It is true that Lafite went through a bad patch beginning in the late 1960s, continuing for about 10 years, but the same can be said of other first growths.

What makes Lafite a particular favourite for many Bordeaux lovers is its wonderful elegance. Winelovers of the old school like to speak about 'breed' in a wine. It has always struck me as a slightly snobbish term, but if it means, as I suspect it does, a blend of elegance, poise, freshness, and distinction, then Lafite, undeniably, has breed.

The estate lies at the northern end of Pauillac, and were it not for the smart blue signs pointing from the head of the driveway to the château itself, it would be easy to miss it altogether when driving from the village of Le Pouyalet to the oriental follies of the *chai* of Château Cos d'Estournel. Indeed the border between Pauillac and Saint-Estèphe, of which Cos is perhaps the leading estate, lies at the northern boundary of Lafite. The ground dips to where a stream idles from west to east. The soil here is too rich for grapes, and this couple of hundred metres offers an uncharacteristic but welcome landscape of meadow, grass, shrubbery, and weeping-willow trees.

The château at Lafite dates from the sixteenth century, but only the turret is of that period. Most of the house is a fairly modest two-storey *manoir*, framed by terraces and balustrades. It remains a family home. The managing director of Lafite, Baron Eric de Rothschild, lives in Paris, but he and his family frequently come to Lafite during holiday periods. His wife is Italian and they have three children. They should feel perfectly at home at the château. Its interior, furnished in Second Empire style, is full of family portraits, photographs, and busts. Much of the history of the Rothschilds' involvement in Pauillac can be traced on the walls of the red and green drawing rooms.

Down in the cellars is the fabulous private collection of older vintages. The oldest wine here is the 1797, a legendary wine and the first vintage to be bottled at the château, and seven bottles remain. Most of the vintages from the 1860s onwards are represented in fair quantities, with at least a dozen bottles. Stocks of nineteenth-century Lafite are by no means exhausted.

Lafite takes its name from the local word *fite,* which means mound. The vineyards rise to a height of 27 metres, which may not sound particularly impressive, but in low-lying Pauillac, that makes it one of the highest spots in the commune. Some sources trace back the existence of a *seigneurie* at Lafite to the Middle Ages, although it is not known whether vines were planted here at that time. As at many other leading estates in the Médoc, vineyards were only planted as a commercial proposition in the seventeenth century.

Lafite's first moment of glory struck at this time. The widow who owned Lafite married Jacques de Ségur, who was already the proprietor of other estates in the region. Their son Alexandre inherited the estate on Ségur's death in 1691. Alexandre had the good sense to marry Marie-Thérèse de Clauzel, the heiress to none other than Château Latour. Thus Alexandre and their son Nicolas-Alexandre developed and managed what would soon become some of the greatest vineyards in France.

Under Nicolas-Alexandre the wines of Lafite became recognised for their quality, not only in France but in England and other countries of Europe. Sir Robert Walpole recorded purchases of Lafite in barrels in 1732 and 1733. It was a favourite wine of Madame de Pompadour at the court of Louis XV. On Ségur's death, in 1755, Lafite and Latour were divided. Lafite remained in the hands of the Ségur family, but the financial recklessness of one of the heirs, Comte Nicolas-Marie-Alexandre, resulted in the estate being put on the market in 1784.

It then passed through the hands of various proprietors, but soon the Revolution engulfed the region and the estate, like so many others, was expropriated. The Ségur family survived the Revolution without serious mishap, but Nicolas-Pierre de Pichard, the former president of the Bordeaux *parlement*, who owned Lafite at this time, was guillotined in 1794. In 1797 Lafite was

The exterior of the chai, Château Lafite-Rothschild

The family house at Lafite-Rothschild

The second-year chai at Lafite-Rothschild, designed by the architect Ricardo Bofill

declared a state property, a *bien national*. It was sold to Jean de Witt for more than two million francs. However, Monsieur de Witt overreached himself and couldn't quite find the money to pay for his purchase. Once again Lafite was on the market, and in 1800 was sold to three Dutch wine merchants, who found steady sales for the wine in Britain as well as in Bordeaux itself. It is possible that de Witt was representing the Dutch syndicate from the start.

At this point the history of Lafite becomes murky. Sixteen years after buying the estate, the Dutchmen sold it to Madame Barbe-Rosalie Lemaire, the estranged wife of the financier Ignace-Joseph Vanlerberghe. In 1821 she in turn sold it, or so she led everyone to believe, to a British banker, Sir Samuel Scott. However, subsequent research into the Lafite archives by Professor René Pijassou and Cyril Ray established that Scott was no more than an absentee caretaker of the estate, which the real owners were seeking to protect from creditors. Madame Lemaire was obliged under French inheritance laws to leave the estate to her children equally. This she did not wish to do so she let it be known that she had sold the property to Scott.

After the death of her favoured son Aimé, who had no children, Lafite was once again on the market. It was by now a very large wine estate, with about 75 hectares in production. Although yields were considerably lower in the nineteenth century than they are today, this still represented a substantial amount of wine.

Lafite underwent expansion during the mid-nineteenth century. Under the Goudal family, who were in effect hereditary managers of the estate, an important parcel of land was acquired called the Carruades, which now gives its name to the second wine of Lafite. Émile Goudal was desperate to get his hands on the Carruades, which, even unplanted, he considered the best *terroir* in all the Médoc. Mouton, too, was after it, and Goudal secured the Carruades just half an hour before Mouton's representatives came through with an improved offer. It was the Goudals who also established the *vinothèque* in the château's cellars, preserving those priceless old bottles for centuries.

On Aimé's death, in 1868, Lafite was auctioned. The new owner, who paid almost five million francs – far higher than the prices previously paid for comparable properties – for the vineyard, buildings, and stock, was Baron James de Rothschild. The Rothschilds knew a good investment when they saw one, and realised that the estate could continue to be a fine source of revenue as long as standards were maintained. Baron James was not to enjoy his new estate for long. He died a few months later,

Ageing the wine in barriques at Lafite-Rothschild

The château's wooden fermentation vats are still in use

without ever having visited Lafite, which his three sons inherited. Ever since, it has remained in the hands of the French Rothschilds, with one member of the family being appointed or invited to assume responsibility for its management.

In 1942 Lafite was occupied by German forces, but the estate itself was expropriated by the Vichy government, which retained the staff and continued to produce wine. Baron Elie, who was the great-grandson of Baron James, was the best known of recent managers of Lafite, and in 1974 he handed over the running of the estate to his nephew Eric, who was then 34 years old. The man on the spot since the 1980s has been Charles Chevallier, who is charged not only with the day-to-day management of Lafite but with looking after some of the Rothschilds' other estates in Bordeaux, namely Château Duhart-Milon in Pauillac, Château L'Evangile in Pomerol, and Château Rieussec in Sauternes.

Lafite is the largest of the great domaines of Pauillac, with about 100 hectares planted with vines. Two-thirds of the vineyards are laid out in a single parcel surrounding the château, including some plots on the eastern side of the D2 road that runs from Pauillac to Saint Estèphe. Other parcels are mingled with the vines of Duhart-Milon to the southwest, while three hectares lie within the boundaries of Saint Estèphe. The vineyards of the Carruades plateau, acquired in 1844, are located in four parcels to the south of the main vineyards of Lafite, and another block is planted just south of the road known as the D4E. Although the Carruades gives its name to the second wine, much of the Cabernet Sauvignon from here is of outstanding quality and frequently finds its way into the *grand vin*. The Merlot from the Carruades is of more variable quality. The southern stretches of the Lafite vineyards adjoin those of its great rival, Château Mouton-Rothschild.

Given the size of the estate, it is not surprising that the soils are quite varied. Gravel predominates, and the very finest parcels, just south of the *chais* on the relatively high plateau of Lafite, have exceptionally deep gravel giving excellent drainage. In most places the gravel is about four metres deep, lying on a bed of marl, which itself reposes on a bed of limestone. Elsewhere there is a clay subsoil, and these vineyards tend to be planted with Merlot. Some of the old drainage channels dating from the nineteenth century have been restored, but the majority have been replaced.

Chevallier and his team are well aware that different plots give different wines, and are placing great emphasis on separate vinifications, allowing them to assess and analyse the variations that exist between the various sites. The *terroir* of Lafite, insists Chevallier, accounts for 90 percent of the wine's quality, and the vineyards are remarkably precocious. The neighbouring property, Château Duhart-Milon, is only a kilometre away from the Lafite *chais*, but its vines mature five to seven days later.

Although not an organic estate, Lafite rarely employs chemical fertilizers, and compost is routinely added instead. As at many traditional estates, each *vigneron*, or vineyard worker, is responsible for his or her own sector of vines. This gives the *vigneron* great pride in the quality of the vines and the skill with which they are pruned. It also helps the *chef de culture* monitor the *vignerons'* care of the vines.

The entrance to the cellars at Lafite-Rothschild

Lafite is dominated by Cabernet Sauvignon. Although Merlot makes up a quarter of the area under vine, its presence in the *grand vin* can vary considerably, depending on its quality in each vintage. In practice its proportion in the blend ranges from 10 to 25 percent.

One of Chevallier's innovations has been to create a new position at Lafite: Eric Kohler has been brought in to propose ways in which quality can be improved. He has been given a free hand to pursue investigations, regardless of cost, as long as the goal is an eventual increase in the quality of the wine. One of his projects has been the analysis of the estate's Petit Verdot. Lafite has always had a small proportion of this occasionally maligned grape variety and recently planted another hectare. Kohler vinifies the Petit Verdot in very small tanks to help him analyse its qualities. It was used in the *grand vin* in 1994 and 1996, but not 1995.

Cabernet Franc has also been planted, and this is a variety that, unlike Petit Verdot, never used to be part of the Lafite blend. In Chevallier's view, Cabernet Franc has the peculiar quality of either being fabulous or useless. 'One can still make decent wine from Cabernet Sauvignon that is not fully ripe, but unripe Cabernet Franc is no good for anything.' Lafite vinifies Cabernet Franc separately and, for the first time in 12 years, used a little in the *grand vin* in 1995 and 1996. Average yields range from 50 to 53 hectolitres per hectare, and green-harvesting takes place during the summer when considered necessary. Before the harvest, all vines younger than 10 years or having some other deficiency are tagged, and these grapes are picked separately at the beginning of the harvest. The pickers then wait for the remaining vines to attain maximum maturity before the entirely manual main harvest begins. The whole of Lafite and Duhart-Milon are usually picked within 12 days. There is a scrupulous *triage à la vigne*. Manual destemming was abandoned some years ago.

There is nothing novel about the vinification, which takes place both in old oak vats and in modern steel tanks. The Lafite team have a fondness for the wooden vats, which retain heat better than the gleaming steel tanks. The drawback, of course, is the cost of maintenance. However, Chevallier admits that he finds very little difference in quality between wines vinified in wood or steel.

Lafite is not especially hi-tech. There is temperature control for each fermentation vat, but decisions about the frequency of *remontage* (pumping over) and length of *cuvaison* are taken on the basis of repeated tastings and analyses. Lafite is equipped with a *concentrateur* (see Introduction) and has made use of the machine since 1990 and 1991. Chevallier believes that it is only of use when the must is balanced. Any false notes will only be accentuated further by the *concentrateur*, so it is only used for the best lots in damp years.

Blending takes place relatively late, usually in March. This means that the blend is made after the wine has begun its *élevage*. Lots destined for the *grand vin* are aged in new oak, whereas Carruades receives only a small proportion of new wood.

The clocktower of Lafite-Rothschild

A distinctive feature of Lafite is that it owns its own cooperage, or *tonnelerie*. Located close to the Duhart-Milon vineyards, it produces all the barrels required for Châteaux Lafite, Duhart-Milon, and Rieussec. The great advantage of having your own cooperage is that you can control the quality, drying, and toasting of the wood far more closely than is possible when ordering from even the best-known French coopers. The Rothschilds buy from two suppliers of woods, using oak from five different forests. The staves are air-dried before being made into barrels.

The wines are aged for 18 to 20 months in new oak. In the 1960s it would have been usual to age the wines for up to three years, but that is no longer done by any estate in the Médoc. The first-year *chai* at Lafite is impressive for its size, but it is the second-year *chai*, completed in 1988, that is more arresting. Designed by the Catalan architect Ricardo Bofill, it is constructed of concrete and is entirely underground. The *chai* has a wonderful atmosphere of silence and repose and is ideal for barrel-ageing. The floor is laid with gravel over earth to ensure good humidity.

Once the *élevage* is complete, the wines are fined with eggwhite, given an extremely light filtration which Chevallier likens to sieving, and are

The immaculately tended vineyards of Château Lafite-Rothschild

bottled in early July. In 1869, according to the late wine connoisseur and historian André Simon, the vintage was, for the first time, château-bottled in its entirety, although this laudable practice was abandoned from 1885 to 1906. About one-third of the production is selected for the *grand vin*, about 40 percent is bottled as Carruades, and the rest is sold as Pauillac. Although the name Carruades refers to a specific vineyard, by no means all the wine called Carruades will come from this sector, and indeed much wine from the Carruades will end up in the *grand vin*. Lafite has toyed over the years with other names for the second wine, such as Moulin des Carruades, but Carruades de Château Lafite has been used since 1985 and is likely to stick. In truly awful vintages – such as 1927, 1930, 1932, 1935, and 1936 – the entire crop was declassified and simply sold as Pauillac. Improved vinification techniques make it unlikely that this will ever happen again.

The commercial structure is slightly peculiar at Lafite: although they work with the usual Bordeaux *négociants*, they also own a small *négociant* company of their own which distributes the third wine, labelled Pauillac.

Lafite has fought hard to retain its reputation as the first of the first growths, as *primus inter pares*. Most experienced tasters, however, will agree that Lafite is not the most consistent of the great wines of Bordeaux. When truly great, Lafite is magical, but it can also disappoint. Less massive and fruity than the other *premiers crus*, it is possible that any faults in the wine are less likely to be masked by tannic weight. Lafite depends on poise and finesse rather than opulence.

A mature Lafite has all the cedary and tobacco notes of an old Pauillac, but there is more than that. There is a silkiness to the wine's texture, an ethereal quality to its aromas, and an unmatchable finesse that mark out a fine Lafite as something extraordinary. It is a wine to be sipped and savoured at great leisure, and as it sits in the glass it often opens up to display ever greater subtlety. In older Lafites that have come my way, I have often discerned aromas and flavours not only of cigar boxes, but of truffles and coffee, of wild strawberries and raspberries. There is a sweetness to the finish on a great Lafite that is seductive yet never cloying. Instead it seems a quintessence of ripe fruit given shapeliness and refinement by the skilful use of new oak.

CHÂTEAU LAFITE-ROTHSCHILD
Area under vine: 100 hectares
Grape varieties: 70% Cabernet Sauvignon, 25% Merlot, 3% Cabernet Franc, 2% Petit Verdot
Average age of vines: 40 years
Director: Charles Chevallier
Technical director: Dominique Befve
Maître de chai: Francis Perez
Chef de culture: J. Paul Baney
Oak ageing: 18-20 months in 100% new oak
Second wine: Carruades de Lafite
Third wine: Pauillac de Château Lafite
Average production: 18,000 cases

Château Latour

CHÂTEAU LATOUR

For many winelovers, Latour is the Pauillac of Pauillacs. In its power, majesty, depth of flavour, and longevity it is unsurpassed by any other wine of the commune. These characteristics have proved remarkably consistent over the years, and the only plausible explanation has to be the exceptional exposition and microclimate of the Latour vineyards.

The estate is also remarkable in that its history has been more thoroughly documented and researched than any other in Pauillac. These studies show how Latour has been an important property since medieval times, and a castle that once stood in the present-day village of Saint Lambert was at the heart of the domaine. The history of Latour is recorded in its vast archives, and detailed accounts have been given in the immense study of the domaine by Professor Charles Higounet.

As at other *seigneuries* that held sway within Pauillac and beyond, that of Latour was run as a major farm, and vineyards were planted within its boundaries. At most estates the vineyards were peripheral to the main economic activity of these farms, but even in the fourteenth and fifteenth centuries the area under vine at Latour was considerable. In the late sixteenth century Arnaud de Mullet transformed Latour from a collection of tenancies to a single, complex agricultural unit. The estate passed to his son Denis, then to Denis's niece. In 1670 Latour was sold to François Chanevas, who left it to his niece, through whom it came into the hands of the De Clauzel family.

By this time the wine of Latour already enjoyed a good reputation. By the early eighteenth century it was being exported to England and Holland at prices comparable to those of Lafite. Alexandre de Ségur had inherited Château Lafite in 1691, and four years later he married Marie-Thérèse de Clauzel. Since she was heiress to Château Latour, Ségur in effect ran the two most important domaines of Pauillac. After Alexandre's death, his son Nicolas-Alexandre inherited both estates, thus acquiring his sobriquet *le prince des vignes*. After his death, in 1755, the two estates were separated, and Latour passed into the control of his descendants. At this time the size of the vineyards was a modest 25 to 30 hectares, and exports to England proved the most profitable side of the enterprise.

By the time of the Revolution in 1789 the principal owners, all married into the Ségur family, were the Comte de la Pallu, Comte de Ségur-Cabanac, and Marquis de Beaumont. Since they all lived in Paris, their estates were run by *régisseurs*. After the Revolution the share of the Comte de Ségur-Cabanac, who had emigrated, was expropriated and sold. In 1841 a limited company was formed, which ensured that the estate remained in the control of the family, although since the 1830s the Bordeaux *négociants*, Nathaniel Barton and Pierre-François

Guestier, were also shareholders. In the 1840s they were bought out by the family. It was also in the 1840s that the descendants of the Ségurs were able to buy back the estate. At this time the principal shareholders were the descendants of the Marquis de Beaumont, and the descendants of the Comte de la Pallu, who were known as the Courtivron family.

In the mid-nineteenth century château-bottling was introduced at Latour, though for only a portion of the crop. It was not until the late 1920s that Latour followed Mouton's lead and began bottling the entire production at the château. At this time Merlot was planted to supplement Cabernet Sauvignon, and varieties such as Syrah, common in Pauillac in the early nineteenth century, were phased out.

The vineyards of Latour did not escape the afflictions of the late nineteenth century. Mildew attacked its vineyards from 1879 to 1887. Phylloxera broke out in the 1880s, but some of the vines proved surprisingly resistant, enabling the remedy of grafting on American rootstocks to take place gradually. In the meantime phylloxera was kept at bay, with some success, by chemical treatments. By the 1920s the entire vineyard had been replanted on American rootstocks. By this time the estate had grown slightly larger and encompassed some 40 hectares of vines. As a result of replanting and missing vines, André Cazes, the former mayor of Pauillac, estimates that yields were no more than 20 hectolitres per hectare.

Under French inheritance laws, shareholders proliferate through succeeding generations, as all the descendants of a co-owner receive an equal share of the property. Shareholders sat tight through the 1930s, when revenues were low, and even after World War II there was no great demand for the superb vintages of 1947 and 1949. Château Latour was sitting on a vast amount of stock.

However, in the 1950s, prices began to rise again as demand increased. By the late 1950s there were some 68 shareholders. For most of them it was not a profitable portfolio since they were rewarded with half a dozen cases of Château Latour annually rather than cash dividends. The current Marquis de Beaumont was keen to hang on to the estate, but was outvoted by the other shareholders. In 1962 the co-owners of Latour sold 51 percent of the estate for £900,000 to the British company Pearsons, whose chairman was Lord Cowdray. Harveys of Bristol, a celebrated wine importer, took a 25 percent share, and about 20 percent was retained by various members of the Beaumont family. Both sides considered they had a bargain deal.

The daily management of the estate was put in the hands of two men: Jean-Paul Gardère, a wine broker, and Henri Martin, the owner of Château Gloria in Saint Julien and a leading publicist for the wines of Bordeaux. Under this new revitalised ownership and management, the vineyards were expanded. Some 12 hectares near Château Batailley, known appropriately as Le Petit Batailley, had been in Latour's hands for years and were now replanted. This was to form the backbone of Latour's second wine, Les Forts de Latour. Other smaller parcels, once part of the estate north of the main vineyards, were also acquired and planted. The Pearsons team discovered that half the vines were missing and although the area under vine was 50 hectares, or so, only half of it was actually in production! Pearsons could have simply replanted from scratch. Instead they decided to replace individual vines, a more difficult and

The walled vineyards at Latour

costly process that took 10 years, but one that conserved the oldest vines. There were innovations at the *chai* too, and in 1964 stainless-steel vats were installed – the first in Bordeaux, other than those at Château Haut-Brion which date from 1961. Destemming was mechanized.

In 1986 Christian Le Sommer was recruited to manage the estate; he had previously been the assistant winemaker at Château d'Yquem. By this time Jean-Paul Gardère had retired but was still a consultant to the estate. He left Latour in 1987 as he and Le Sommer did not always see eye to eye. Henri Martin left the same year.

In the late 1980s, when Bordeaux was enjoying a boom period, events moved rapidly at Latour. Harveys was now owned by a much larger company, Allied-Lyons, which in turn bought the 53 percent Pearsons' stake and most of the shares remaining in the hands of the Beaumont family. In the 27 years since the Pearsons' purchase, the value of Latour had increased a hundredfold. Nonetheless, soon after Allied-Lyons acquired this prestigious estate, the group suffered from currency losses and decided to put Latour on the market in November 1992. A spokesman at the time pointed out that returns had been disappointing, suggesting that Allied

ABOVE: *An architectural detail, Château Latour*

OPPOSITE: *The château's landmark seventeenth-century dovecot*

Lyons did not regard the purchase as a long-term investment. Naturally there was keen interest in Latour from a variety of sources, but eventually, in June of 1993, it was sold to a company called Artemis, owned by the industrialist François Pinault, for 735 million francs. Château Latour was back in French hands.

François Pinault was clearly in no hurry to make changes at Latour. Living in Paris, he was content to leave the daily management of the estate in the hands of the team that had worked for Allied-Lyons. From time to time various economies were proposed that would not affect the quality of the wine. For example, it was suggested that the individual wrapping of every bottle in tissue paper could be abandoned; and that top-quality long corks could be substituted, without any diminution in ageing potential, for the ultra-long corks previously favoured at Latour. Pinault rejected both suggestions. Latour remained unchanged.

There is not much to see at Latour. The château, designed by the Bordeaux architect Théodore Duphot, is maintained but rarely occupied, and it is not one of Pauillac's more distinctive houses. The offices and *chais* are modest, too, though superbly equipped. Easily the most stylish landmark at Latour is the famous tower, a dovecot dating from the 1620s.

It's the vineyards that make Latour what it is, arguably the finest red wine of the Médoc. For Bordeaux lovers it is awe-inspiring to stand on top of the *croupe* at Latour and know that some truly great wines have emerged from this stony *terroir*. The core of the Latour holdings are around the château and *chais*: a parcel, either walled or bounded by streams, called L'Enclos, with an area of 45 hectares. The total area under vine at Latour is 65 hectares in three principal parcels.

To the south of L'Enclos, a stream called Jaille de Juillac separates Latour's vineyards from those of the great Saint Julien vineyard of Léoville-Las Cases. Northwest of the château and just west of L'Enclos is another parcel where Pearsons planted vines from 1963 to 1988; much of this wine is used for Les Forts. The third major parcel is composed of two lots, Le Petit Batailley and La Pinada, both planted in 1963 and situated close to the vineyards of the two Pichon estates. These total 18 hectares, which give wine that is extremely good but usually lacks the profundity of that from L'Enclos, a vineyard of stony gravel above a subsoil of gravel and clay mixed with sand, all of which rests on a bed of clay. Petit Batailley is on finer gravel. Seventy percent of the soil at the top of L'Enclos is stones, so it is truly impoverished and needs occasional additions of compost to nourish the vines.

Latour's technical director, Christian Le Sommer, explains: 'The *grand vin* invariably comes from L'Enclos. There are some vintages when we

Ivy and lichen at Latour

taste the wine from Petit Batailley and La Pinada and we are highly impressed. But experience has taught us that although these wines can taste excellent young, they never evolve as superbly as those from L'Enclos. To me this is a convincing proof of the supremacy of *terroir*. There is no difference in the viticulture or winemaking – though it is the case that we have a higher proportion of Merlot at Petit Batailley, which tends to be flattering when young – yet the vines of L'Enclos always emerge triumphant.'

The explanation may lie in the deep gravel soil and its exemplary drainage, but also in the microclimate. Of all the major vineyards in Pauillac, this is the one that lies closest to the Gironde. Three hundred metres of fields are all that separate the vines from the river and estuary. Over the course of a year, L'Enclos is half a degree warmer than the other vineyards of Pauillac, giving more precocious vines. Moreover, the stony topsoil reflects heat onto the vines during the summer, further assisting their ripening.

Because of its milder climate, the vines of L'Enclos flower earlier. The Latour harvesters usually pick L'Enclos eight to ten days earlier than Petit Batailley, a remarkable difference considering that only two kilometres separate the vineyards. This precocity means that in certain years, when the harvest is marred by rain, L'Enclos has already been picked, allowing Château Latour to make a very good wine when other properties are struggling to do so.

There are some very old vines at Latour. In 1956 Le Petit Batailley was wiped out by the devastating frost of that year, but L'Enclos was only lightly affected, thanks to its proximity to the waters of the Gironde and the milder microclimate. During the frost of 1985 no vines were lost at Latour. When, in 1991, the Médoc lost 70 percent of the crop to frost, Latour lost only 30 percent. When there is severe frost there is usually a second generation of buds. However, these ripen late as they get off to a late start, and rarely give satisfactory wine. In 1991 Petit Batailley was cropped from second-generation growths, and the entire crop was used for the third wine, the simple Pauillac. In L'Enclos, however, the crop was entirely first-generation, and Château Latour was one of the only estates in Pauillac to find it necessary to green-harvest in 1991, when most of the neighbouring properties were desperate to find a reasonable quantity of usable bunches.

Drainage at Latour is exceptional too. When Pearsons took over in the 1960s, many of the old nineteenth-century drainage channels were cleaned and restored. Since the gravel soils lie on a bed of clay there is good water retention. In very dry years, such as 1990 and 1995, the roots

The entrance to Château Latour

draw water up from the clay. Nonetheless a few vines did suffer from the drought, since the very wet spring in 1995 killed off some root structures that became water-logged, sending roots back up to the surface where they became vulnerable to the shortage of water during summer.

Latour is dominated by Cabernet Sauvignon. About 78 percent of the vineyards are planted with the variety. The density of plantation is 10,000 vines per hectare, and the *chef de culture* replaces individual vines when necessary rather than replanting an entire vineyard. Latour has made a fairly detailed study of the clones in its vineyard, but Christian Le Sommer finds little difference between the clones they have planted and the selections they have propagated in the Latour nurseries from their own vines. The advantage of clonal selections is that the vines are guaranteed to be healthy.

Some 200 pickers are used during the harvest, and *triage* takes place in the vineyard. The must is fermented in stainless-steel tanks at up to 31 degrees Centigrade and the *cuvaison* lasts about one month. By December the wine is ready to go into *barriques*, where it stays for 20 months. Pneumatic presses have improved the quality of the press wine, which in the past often contributed awesome tannins. Most of the blending of the *grand vin* is done just before the wine goes into *barriques*, but there is a further blending in March when the press wine is added. Although Latour has experimented with malolactic fermentation in *barriques*, it continues to allow most of the wine to go through this process in vats. The first-year *chai* dates from the nineteenth century but was extended in 1988; the second-year *chai* is underground and enjoys a steady temperature of between 12 and 14 degrees Centigrade.

The *grand vin* is always aged in new oak, but lots such as those from young vines that the Latour team knows in advance will never be part of the *grand vin* are aged in 50 percent new oak. There is talk of reducing the time spent in oak from 20 months to 18, but no final decision has been taken. The wines that will end up as the third wine, the Pauillac, are aged in three-year-old *barriques*. Latour uses 10 different coopers as a security measure, preferring wood from the Allier forests with a medium toast, though they have discovered that each cooper offers a slightly different interpretation of 'medium'. Latour has always used new oak, but in the nineteenth century the oak came from the Baltic forests and was crafted at the estate's own cooperage; young wines not sold to *négociants* were usually kept in *barriques* at the *chais* for at least four years.

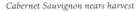

Cabernet Sauvignon nears harvest

'By appointment only' is the rule at Latour

The wines are fined with eggwhite but bottled without filtration. Until 1970 eight *barriques* were blended at a time before bottling; thereafter there has been a more thorough homogenizing of the wine to reduce the risk of bottle variation. It is hard to generalize, but roughly 55 percent of the crop will probably end up as the *grand vin*, 35 percent as Les Forts, and the rest as Pauillac. The Pauillac is usually bottled in May, Les Forts in June, and Latour in July.

Les Forts de Latour, first made in 1966, is one of the outstanding second wines of Pauillac. Curiously it can often taste more oaky when young than the *grand vin*, probably because its less structured fruit is more easily infused with oaky flavours. Much of the wine that goes into Les Forts comes from Petit Batailley, and it also includes lots that have been declassified during tastings in the *chai*. As the vines of Petit Batailley have reached maturity, so Les Forts has become a more impressive wine in its own right.

The château used to have an admirable policy of only releasing Les Forts when it was ready to drink, and 1989 was the last vintage of which this was true. Since 1993 Les Forts has been offered *en primeur* together with the *grand vin*. Christian Le Sommer explains that it was too confusing to continue with two different marketing strategies for the wines from a single estate. He also believes that the existence of a third wine, labeled Pauillac, will further improve the quality of Les Forts. This may be true, but the logic is doubtful, since the process could be elongated indefinitely, producing fourth and fifth wines for the same reason. There is a growing trend towards third wines at the top estates, which seems to be a marketing device to

Autumn harvest near Latour

justify increasing the prices of second wines. Latour's 'Pauillac' was first made in 1973, then again in 1974 and 1987; since 1990 the wine has been made systematically.

The style of Latour used to be uncompromising: rich, almost heavy, and always profoundly structured, with mighty tannins sustaining a core of fruit. These were wines that could take 20 years to come round. That certainly seemed to be true of the great 1970, which remained dormant and unyielding for ages. It is a great strength of Latour, when comparing it with the other first growths, to note how often the wine succeeds in poor vintages such as 1968 and 1974. This is probably a consequence of the vineyard's precocity.

Latour is less feline and elegant than Lafite, less voluptuous than Mouton. It avoids the excesses of both the other two first growths, and is arguably the most classic wine of Pauillac. A good Latour is a deeply satisfying wine, darkly coloured, full-flavoured yet elegant, densely structured, muscular yet noble and persistent in flavour, developing remarkable complexity of aroma, flavour, and texture as it ages.

CHÂTEAU LATOUR
Area under vine: 65 hectares
Grape varieties: 78% Cabernet Sauvignon, 16% Merlot, plus Cabernet Franc and Petit Verdot
Average age of vines: 45 years
Director and winemaker: Christian Le Sommer
Maître de chai: Denis Malbec
Chef de culture: Frédéric Ardouin
Oak ageing: 20 months in 100% new oak
Second wine: Les Forts de Latour
Third wine: Pauillac de Château Latour
Average production: 18,500 cases

The entrance post at Latour, displaying the property's familiar emblem

Château Mouton-Rothschild

CHÂTEAU MOUTON-ROTHSCHILD

Premier je suis. Second je fus. Mouton ne change. This was the defiant motto adopted by Baron Philippe de Rothschild after his decades-long campaign to have Mouton upgraded from second to first-growth status finally succeeded in 1973. The swagger has to be admired, with its clear implication that Mouton was always in reality a first growth, even if the authorities in 1855 had failed to notice. The baron was of course quite right. Mouton was always reputed to be on the same quality level as Lafite and Latour and often matched the prices of its illustrious neighbours.

Not a great deal is known of the early history of Mouton. *Motte*, from which Mouton is probably derived, means mound. These modest eminences were always known to be the places where the gravel was at its deepest and gave the best wines. In the eighteenth century the owner was Joseph de Brane, a member of the Bordeaux *noblesse de la robe*. When he acquired a house near the village of Le Pouyalet, the property was part of the barony of Mouton, entitling him to attach that name to his vineyards.

By the end of the eighteenth century its wines were fetching prices similar to those obtained by the Pichon vineyards – in other words, second-growth prices – but the de Brane family worked hard to improve the quality of the wine even further. It was widely recognized that they succeeded, yet in 1830 the property was put up for sale. By this time about 50 hectares were under vine. The purchaser, Isaac Thuret, was one of the first Parisian bankers to venture into the Médoc. Although he paid a substantial price for the estate, it appears that he did not match his initial investment with a commitment to improving or even maintaining quality, and this may account for Mouton's relatively poor showing in 1855, even though Mouton's wine usually fetched the same price as Lafite.

Two years before the classification, Thuret sold Brane-Mouton, then with 37 hectares of vineyards, to Baron Nathaniel de Rothschild of the English branch of the banking dynasty, for much the same sum as he had paid for it some 20 years earlier. Although Baron Nathaniel never lived at Mouton – the only buildings that may have been habitable belonged to the neighbouring estate of Armailhacq – he spent much of the remaining 17 years of his life improving the condition of the vines and the quality of the wine. He was assisted locally by his *régisseur* Théodore Galos. At this time Mouton was already an estate dominated by Cabernet Sauvignon, as it remains today.

After the death of Baron Nathaniel, in 1870, the property was inherited by his son James, who a decade later built the very modest château, now called Le Petit Mouton and standing,

The oak fermentation vats, still in service at Mouton-Rothschild

somewhat incongruously, in the middle of the courtyard surrounded by the *chais* and other buildings. James died in his thirties in 1881, but his widow, Laura Thérèse, took over and ran the estate until her own death, 40 years later, in 1920.

Madame Thérèse seems to have run Mouton capably, despite the fact that she was a teetotaler and presumably never drank the wine. Her elder son Henri inherited Mouton but showed little interest in the estate and was willing to stand aside when his younger brother Philippe decided to occupy himself with its management. It was many years later, in 1947, that Philippe bought out his sibling's shares in the estate and became principal proprietor.

When Baron Philippe arrived at Mouton in 1922 he was 20 years old. Within two years he made a profound innovation: the entire 1924 vintage was bottled at the château. It would be a few years before the other first growths followed suit, and as late as the 1970s other classified growths were still shipping their wines in barrel to the Bordeaux *négociants*. He also began making improvements both to the living quarters and the winery buildings. The architect Charles Siclis was invited to construct the still-impressive first-year *chai*.

At this time Baron Philippe was a mere 22-year old and not one to harbour self-doubts. He had already developed a passion for literature, the theatre, and the arts. Having bottled his wine in 1924, he had the audacity to put on it a Cubist-style label designed by the artist Jean Carlu. In 1933 the baron bought Château Mouton-d'Armailhacq, not only for the vines but because, unlike Mouton itself, it had the vestiges of a château and an attractive park.

Another innovation was the creation of a second wine into which the less satisfactory lots of Mouton and (after 1933) d'Armailhacq were consigned. This was Mouton-Cadet, which first appeared in the early 1930s as a response to the poor 1930 vintage. Without any change of name, the wine became a branded Bordeaux, with negligible or even nonexistent relation to the classified growths. The name was a clever marketing ploy, giving to this day the spurious impression that there is some connection between Mouton-Cadet and the distinguished first growth.

The baron was lucky to survive the war. His property was expropriated, he was deprived of his French citizenship, and imprisoned. He managed to escape from France to Britain, but his wife was less fortunate: she died in a German concentration camp in 1945. Like other châteaux in Pauillac, Mouton was occupied by the German army. The *Weinführer* ensured that the cellars were left untouched and the estate continued to produce fine wine. After the war Baron Philippe returned to Mouton. In 1954 he remarried. His new wife was an American, Pauline Fairfax-Potter. To the enduring grief of the baron, she died in 1976.

Baron Philippe's energetic devotion to Mouton was motivated by his determination to see the estate promoted to the first growths. He knew, as did everyone else who had followed the wines of the leading châteaux of Pauillac, that Mouton was the equal of the first growths, and he wanted that fact recognized. It took him half a century, but eventually he succeeded and it was a future president of the republic, Jacques Chirac, who signed the decree.

Details of oak vats at Mouton-Rothschild

Baron Philippe, unlike many other proprietors of Pauillac estates, was no absentee landlord. He was profoundly involved in running Mouton and indeed did his best to turn it into a tourist attraction. Visitors have long been welcome to the estate, and there is a special visitors' reception centre, to which admission is charged and where tours of Mouton begin. Only in recent years has the central part of the property been fenced off to prevent over-enthusiastic tourists from wandering into the private quarters of the present owner, Baroness Philippine de Rothschild, Baron Philippe's daughter.

The baron created a superlative museum of artifacts relating to wine, and initiated a brilliantly successful tradition of commissioning some of the world's best-known artists to produce works reproduced exclusively on the Mouton label. Even more remarkably, he persuaded these artists to

do so in exchange for a mere 10 cases of the wine. Some of the reception halls are decorated with tapestries and other items from the Rothschild collections. All this is a far cry from the discretion and relative aloofness of Mouton's rivals.

Since Baron Philippe's death, in 1988, the estate has been managed by his daughter Philippine, an actress who inherited much of her father's flamboyance and love of publicity. She has maintained her father's bold ventures, such as his cooperative winemaking with Robert Mondavi, and is an exuberant ambassador for the wines of Mouton.

Château Mouton-Rothschild is a large estate, though slightly smaller than its neighbour Lafite. Some 80 percent of the vineyard is planted with Cabernet Sauvignon. The gravel soil is exceptionally deep, some eight metres in places, and lies on a bed of larger stones mixed with sand, whereas far below the subsoil is of clay and limestone. The majority of the vines lie to the south of Lafite's, with parcels on the same Carruades made famous by Lafite's second wine. There are some vines that are over a century old, and Mouton prefers to replace individual vines that are diseased or no longer productive, rather than eradicate entire parcels. The use of chemicals and fertilizers is kept to an absolute minimum in the vineyards. Vines are planted to a density of about 8,000 vines per hectare.

One curiosity at Mouton is the presence of four hectares of white grape varieties from which a white wine is produced. Some of the vines were planted in 1985 and others were grafted onto existing red vines. The usual blend in the finished wine is 50 percent Semillon, 48 percent Sauvignon Blanc, and 2 percent Muscadelle. The 1991, the first vintage of the wine known as Aile d'Argent, yielded 7,500 bottles of a rather oaky wine. The average yield is about 40 hectolitres per hectare and the maximum production will be 15,000 bottles. Aile d'Argent is fermented and aged for 12 months in new oak, and for about half that time the wine remains on its fine lees.

It is the policy of the Mouton estates (including Clerc-Milon and d'Armailhac) to consign fruit from vines of under 15 years to the second wines. These grapes are picked and vinified separately. The Mouton harvesting team picks the grapes at the Rothschilds' two other Pauillac estates as well so there is maximum flexibility; picking dates are organized to ensure that only the ripest grapes are harvested. The first vines to be harvested are almost always the Merlot, and these tend to be picked by Mouton's own *vignerons*. The Cabernet and other grapes are left to ripen further, at which point the teams of part-time harvesters move in and get to work. Each team is headed by a Mouton *vigneron*, who knows the vines intimately and monitors the

The lobby and entrance to the chai at Mouton-Rothschild

The first-year chai at Mouton-Rothschild ·

harvesting. In wet years, such as 1992, leaves are removed from around the bunches to improve aeration and prevent attacks of grey rot and other maladies. There is *triage* in the vineyard and again when the grapes arrive at the winery. Mouton is the last of the Pauillac estates to destem by hand, though this is not done to the whole crop. The value of destemming is that unripe grapes, which are not easily removed from their stalks, are eliminated.

The must is fermented in 27 wooden vats of 220 hectolitres each, and the winemakers are not afraid to allow the temperature to rise to 33 degrees Centigrade. I was slightly surprised that the temperature of most of the vats rose so high, but that can give excellent extraction from healthy fruit, which was certainly the case in 1996. If the autumn is warm, the wine can be cooled by passing it through a heat exchanger.

The *cuvaison* is fairly long, about four weeks. The *marc* is pressed in hydraulic presses, which are slow to operate but give wine of high quality. The wine is blended shortly after the malolactic fermentation is completed. About 15 percent of the malolactic is undergone in barrels, the remainder in tanks. Hervé Berland believes that this helps the wine taste more appealing when young but has no long-term effect on its ageing potential.

For its first year the new vintage is lodged in architect Charles Siclis's magnificent *chai*, which can house up to 1,000 barrels. Mouton orders its barrels from eight different coopers to minimize any shortcomings in the barrel-making process. All barrels are new and use medium-toasted wood from the Tronçais forest. The second-year *chai* is underground, dark, dank, and humid. Towards the end of the *élevage* the wine is fined with eggwhites, then given a rough filtration before bottling.

Leading off from the second-year *chai* are two galleries containing the private reserves of the Rothschild family. One contains mostly Mouton, the oldest bottles being from 1859, though I was more tempted by the jeroboams of 1945 slumbering on one of the racks. The other gallery contains a mind-blowing collection of Bordeaux wines, including magnums of Yquem from the 1920s, 1891 Haut-Brion, and dozens of other rarities.

Mouton was the last of the major châteaux in Pauillac to introduce a second wine (apart from the short-lived Mouton-Cadet before its transformation into a brand). In 1993 I asked Philippe Cottin, then the general director of the estate he had been associated with for 40 years, about this policy. He explained that, in his view, although having a second wine allowed estates to be very selective by excluding substandard wines from the *grand vin*, it also encouraged them to write off those parcels unlikely to make it into the *grand vin*. He felt that the lack of a second wine encouraged the *chef de culture* to produce the best possible fruit from all parcels, since he knew there was no dumping ground for unsatisfactory lots.

I'm not sure this argument had a great deal of merit, since there would always be parcels – notably very young vines – that, however skilled the viticulture, would never make it into the top blend. A year later, however, Mouton launched a second wine from the 1993 vintage, called simply Le Second Vin de Mouton. Another was released from the 1994 vintage, but Hervé Berland says it is unlikely that this will be done every year.

Mouton-Rothschild at its best is the most opulent of Pauillacs: a rich mouthful of ripe Cabernet Sauvignon, luxuriously cushioned in new oak. Even in its youth it takes on some of the character of an evolved Pauillac, those cedarwood or cigar-box aromas and flavours that can be so seductive. There is exuberant cassis fruit, and an oakiness that is supported by this depth of vivid fruit. Mouton stands midway in style between Lafite's elegance and Latour's massiveness, an exemplary stylistic compromise offering lush fruit as well as finesse.

The exterior of the chai and museum at Mouton-Rothschild

CHÂTEAU MOUTON-ROTHSCHILD
Area under vine: 80 hectares
Grape varieties: 80% Cabernet Sauvignon, 8% Merlot,
10% Cabernet Franc, 2% Petit Verdot
Average age of vines: 45 years
Directors: Patrick Léon and Hervé Berland
Winemaker: Patrick Léon
Maître de chai: Eric Tourbier
Chef de culture: Gilles Rey
Oak ageing: 18-20 months in 100% new oak
Second wine: Le Second Vin de Mouton
Average production: 26,000 cases

It seems no coincidence that Baron Philippe, quite late in life, teamed up with the man who was his equivalent in Napa Valley, another man of charisma, endless curiosity, rare showmanship, and a striving for quality whatever the cost: Robert Mondavi. Together they created Opus One, a Médoc-style Napa Cabernet, using, for instance, the density of planting in Pauillac rather than the wider rows encountered in California.

Mouton is indeed the most Californian of Pauillacs. This is not faint praise, as there is no doubt that Napa Valley has produced some of the world's greatest Cabernet-based wines. I once participated in a blind tasting that compared Mouton-Rothschild, Mondavi's Reserve Cabernet, and Opus One in three different vintages. The Reserve Cabernet, in my view and also that of other participants, was often superior to Opus One and close in quality to Mouton. It was by no means easy to tell the wines apart. It is this opulence and fleshiness that Mouton and some top Napa Cabernets have in common. Mouton may lack the sheer finesse of Lafite or Pichon-Lalande, but it is a wine for sensualists, a sumptuous mouthful that can give the deepest pleasure.

This is not to say that Mouton is a wine to be drunk young. Although its succulence makes it more accessible in its youth than, say, a Latour of the same vintage, it is a wine built for the long haul, often closing up after a burst of youthful exuberance and offering after 20 years or so in bottle that high-powered cedary silkiness that is the hallmark of Mouton.

Mouton-Rothschild's landmark spire

Glass marbles on island in reflecting pond, Château Longueville au Baron de Pichon-Longueville

The Second Growths

⁓

CHÂTEAUX

Pichon-Longueville, Comtesse de Lalande • Longueville au Baron de Pichon-Longueville

Château Pichon-Longueville, Comtesse de Lalande

There are two second growths in Pauillac, and they used to form a single estate. The property belonged to the Pichon-Longueville family until 1850, when it was divided among the heirs. By 1860 amalgamations and bequests had created, in effect, two properties from the original estate. Since they both belonged to different branches of the same Pichon family until the early twentieth century, it became customary to refer to the estates as Pichon-Baron and Pichon-Lalande.

The full title of Pichon-Lalande is Pichon-Longueville, Comtesse de Lalande, and this appears on the label of the grand vin. Across the road, AXA Millésimes use the full title on their labels of Château Longueville au Baron de Pichon-Longueville, often now referred to as Pichon-Longueville. As these are cumbersome formulas to repeat in a book, I hope the proprietors of both estates will forgive my adoption of the shorter titles of Pichon-Lalande and Pichon-Longueville.

~

CHÂTEAU PICHON-LONGUEVILLE, COMTESSE DE LALANDE

The wine of Pichon-Lalande has become one of the best loved, and most expensive, of Pauillac. Its elegance and beauty may, in some eyes, make it atypical of the commune, but just about everyone who has had the fortune to taste a fine vintage of this estate has found it irresistible.

The Pichon estate, which until 1850 was a single domaine, lies in the southern part of Pauillac between the village of Saint Lambert and the boundary with Saint Julien. Today the two châteaux – Pichon-Lalande and Pichon-Longueville – face each other, separated by the D2 road. The Pichon estate lies mostly to the west of the road, and almost all the vines hugging the château and *chais* of Pichon-Lalande belong to Château Latour.

The Pichon family can be traced to the fourteenth century, though details in the family archives are not very informative. In the late sixteenth century the owner of the estate was François de Pichon, whose son Bernard was born in 1602. In 1646 Bernard married Anne, the only daughter of the Baron de Longueville. At this point the Pichons seem to have assumed the title of baron, which would otherwise have become extinct on the death of François.

A crucial alliance was made in 1694 when Jacques de Pichon-Longueville, an important figure who became the president of the Bordeaux *parlement*, married Thérèse de Rauzan. She was the daughter of Pierre de Mazure de Rauzan, and it was he who had made the purchases that evolved into the Pichon domaine. Documents in the archives at Pichon-Lalande include the deeds of his vineyard purchases in 1689; the estate was further consolidated by exchanges of parcels of vines made with Château Latour.

The drawing room at Château Pichon-Lalande

The small wine museum at Pichon-Lalande

The reputation of the vineyard was soon established, and by the mid-eighteenth century its wines were fetching high prices comparable with those of Mouton. After Jacques' death, in 1731, he was succeeded by his son of the same name. Jacques the younger had a son called Jean-Pierre, the father of Joseph, and a key figure in the evolution of the estate.

Some sources give Joseph's date of birth as 1755, but a document in the Pichon-Lalande archives cites the date as 1760. It is not of great importance. What does matter is that Joseph de Pichon-Longueville lived to a ripe old age, dying in 1850 and witnessing through the decades all the great events of the Revolution and the Napoleonic era. During the Revolution Joseph was arrested and imprisoned but released on the condition that 'Citoyen Joseph', as contemporary documents refer to him, did not emigrate.

Joseph had seven children, five of whom were still alive at the time of his death. It was at this point that the estate was divided – not only the vineyards, but the woods and fields. Each child received a share of one-fifth, but his eldest son died soon after, so his share was added to that inherited by the second son Raoul. The remaining three-fifths, including 42 hectares of vines, was bequeathed to the three daughters.

In the gardens of Pichon-Lalande

One of these daughters was the Vicomtesse de Lavaur; a second, the Comtesse Marie-Laure-Virginie de Lalande, usually known more simply as Virginie; the third and eldest, Sophie, was an artist. A pair of paintings by Sophie, now in the château, show her self-portrayed as a slender girl in white sitting by a gushing torrent alongside her beau. The second picture shows her alone, in black, sitting by the same torrent. Clearly her lover had died. Perhaps as a consequence of this sad event, Sophie retreated into a nunnery, bequeathing her vines to her sister, the Comtesse de Lalande. The pious Sophie also painted a *Descent from the Cross* for the inauguration of the church at Pauillac, in which it still hangs.

Raoul de Pichon-Longueville's share of the estate included the *manoir* of La Baderne. It was a modest house and he proposed extending it and erecting *chais* along its side. Although plans were drawn up, he changed his mind and had the *manoir* razed; in its place, in 1851, he built the present château of Pichon-Longueville. Meanwhile, in the 1840s, Virginie commissioned the Bordeaux architect Théodore Duphot to design what is now Château Pichon-Lalande in order to live close to her father.

By 1855 there were 80 hectares under vine at the two properties, forming a sizeable estate. After Raoul's death, in 1860, Virginie decided that the daughters' part of the estate should henceforth be run as a separate domaine. At this point the division between the two Pichon estates became final. Virginie increased her control over the daughters'

Winter pruning in the vineyard

holdings when her sisters died and left their shares to her. Virginie died in 1882 and the Pichon-Lalande estate passed to her niece Elisabeth, who also married a member of the Lalande family.

The estate remained in the hands of the family until 1926. On the death of Comtesse Sophie de Lacroix, her children, in conjunction with her unmarried elder sister Henriette de Lalande, decided to sell the property. The purchaser was the Miailhe family, who paid 700,000 francs for the estate. The Miailhes were already well entrenched in the Médoc, and were (and still are) the owners of Châteaux Verdignan and Coufran.

Édouard Miailhe died in 1959, and William-Alain Miailhe took over the management of the property until a serious disagreement, in 1972, led to his departure. At the time of Édouard Miailhe's death the estate consisted of some 40 hectares in production, but in the 1960s additional parcels were added, including some hectares in Saint Julien.

In 1975 Michel Delon of Château Léoville-Las Cases was invited to manage Pichon-Lalande. In 1978 the family co-ownership was split and Édouard Miailhe's daughter, May-Eliane, inherited the majority shares. She was married to General Hervé de Lenquesaing, who helped her buy out the other partners, giving them virtually complete control of the estate. The Lencquesaings immediately passed on the property to their four children to ease inheritance problems. After the death of General de Lencquesaing, in 1990, his widow asked his nephew, Comte Gildas d'Ollone, to assist her in running the commercial affairs of the estate. In 1997, Madame de Lencquesaing bought the estate of Château Bernadotte, part of which is located within Pauillac as a *cru bourgeois*.

The château had been neglected in the postwar years. Madame de Lencquesaing, never at a loss for energy, set about restoring the heating and water supplies, and the interior of the château, basing her decoration on her memories of the salons before their deterioration. She clearly has an excellent eye, for she has skillfully combined the original furniture with bold modern fabrics and paints. Mouldings have been painted a jazzy kind of marbling and there are striking flower-patterned fabrics on the chairs and sofas of jet-black wood.

Behind the château, on the river side of the house, she has laid out a lovely balustraded lawn and terrace above the *chais*. The whole property is now in immaculate condition and is one of the few that actively welcomes visitors (preferably by appointment), offering tours and an opportunity to buy wines. There is also a small museum of glassware, *tastevins*, and other wine-related objects, not on the scale of the wine museum at Mouton-Rothschild, but nonetheless a most enjoyable collection.

Vineyards near Pichon-Lalande

The chai at Pichon-Lalande

Women have rarely been dominant figures in the Bordeaux wine trade. There is no equivalent to Veuve Clicquot (the Champagne house guided by the legendary Madame Veuve Clicquot Ponsardin from 1805 to 1866), and even today the number of women winemakers in the Médoc can be counted on the fingers of one hand. However, as Madame de Lencquesaing delights in pointing out, Pichon-Lalande has often been run by women, notably Virginie de Lalande, and now herself. Madame de Lencquesaing is one of the dominant personalities of Pauillac. With her forthright views, her ambition, and her competitiveness, she has earned herself some hostility. But no one can dispute the fact that she has done wonders for her estate, restoring its grandeur and beauty and improving the quality of the wine to such an extent that there are vintages when it rivals or matches some of the first growths.

Today the estate consists of 75 hectares in production. For nearly 20 years the estate was run by the *régisseur*, Jean-Jacques Godin, *chef de culture* from 1970 before becoming *régisseur* in 1975. Matters came to a dramatic conclusion when he was fired in 1992, followed a year later by *maître de chai* Francis Lopez. The details are murky, but it appears that Madame de Lencquesaing was unhappy with the whole notion of a *régisseur* capable of accumulating and wielding excessive power, especially with modern proprietors increasingly obliged to travel the world to market their wines. Moreover, police raids on the property in 1992 had unearthed unacceptable winemaking practices, which provided the pretext for the dismissals.

Madame de Lencquesaing promptly restructured the staffing of the estate. A crucial appointment was that of a new technical director, the youthful Franco-Vietnamese Thomas

The winemaking buildings at Pichon-Lalande with Latour's dovecot in background

Dô-Chi-Nam, a graduate of the universities of Dijon and Montpellier. No one disputes that he is overseeing the production of wines of the highest quality.

Given Pauillac's reputation within Bordeaux as the standard bearer for Cabernet Sauvignon, a peculiarity of Pichon-Lalande is its relatively high proportion of Merlot. A mere 45 percent is planted with Cabernet Sauvignon, while 35 percent is devoted to Merlot. Pichon-Lalande is also unusual in retaining a significant proportion of Petit Verdot, some eight percent. Most estates are not replanting this variety on the grounds that it ripens late and is usually more trouble than it is worth. But in the view of Madame de Lencquesaing, it contributes elegance and complexity to the blend, as well as colour and structure. It may well be that it is a useful component precisely because the proportion of Cabernet Sauvignon is relatively small. However, there have been vintages, such as 1995, when no Petit Verdot was included in the blend. The 1996 is also an atypical vintage, since the *grand vin* had a Cabernet Sauvignon content of 70 percent.

Almost all the vines surrounding the château on the river side of the D2 belong to Château Latour, though a single hectare is part of the Pichon-Lalande *vignoble*. The rest of the vineyards lie in large parcels, both to the south of Pichon-Longueville as far as (and indeed across) the border with Saint Julien and just west of the village of Saint Lambert. Although nine hectares lie within the commune of Saint Julien, the château has a special dispensation to allow its production to be included within the Pauillac appellation. Before 1959 it was, apparently, bottled separately under the Saint Julien appellation, though I have never laid eyes on a bottle.

The oldest vines at Pichon-Lalande were planted in the 1930s, and the usual density is some 9,000 vines per hectare. The soil is gravelly, over a base of clay and sandstone, with a layer of limestone beneath that. There is a high iron content in these vineyards, just as there is at Latour.

The entire crop is harvested by hand by up to 150 pickers. *Triage* takes place in the vineyard. Until the mid-1980s the wine was fermented in cement vats, but these have been replaced with stainless-steel tanks. Since 1991, Pichon-Lalande has been equipped with a *concentrateur*, but Madame de Lencquesaing downplays its importance in the vinification, describing it as rather slow and unreliable. The *cuvaison* lasts from 18 to 24 days. The malolactic fermentation takes place in the steel tanks, and then the wine is blended in December before it is poured into barrels. In 1982 one of the *chais à barriques* was extended to an impressive 100 metres and an additional *chai,* now used for the first-year wines, was built in 1986-87. Each has a capacity of 1,500 barrels bought from a number of different coopers.

Only 50 percent new oak is used for the *grand vin* because, in the view of Madame de Lencquesaing, the high Merlot content of the wine would not support a higher proportion. Certainly Pichon-Lalande never seems an excessively oaky wine, and this aspect of the *élevage* appears perfectly judged. The second wine, Réserve de la Comtesse, is aged in 25 percent new oak. Both wines are aged between 18 and 22 months. Fining is traditional, with eggwhites, and the wines are bottled in June.

The second wine, which was introduced in the early 1970s, is essentially a parcel selection of young vines, and there is now a third wine, Domaines des Gartieux, which is produced from the very youngest vines, but this only accounts for about 1,000 cases of the château's production. Madame de Lencquesaing recalls that there used to be a second wine at the estate in the 1880s, but after phylloxera and the subsequent replanting of the vineyards, there ceased to be any justification for a second wine.

Pichon-Lalande is one of the most hedonistic of Pauillacs. Despite its proximity to Latour, the two wines are not alike, and Pichon-Lalande does not aspire to the massive structure and imposing tannins of that first growth. Indeed, if it resembles any of the first growths, it is Lafite. It is an exceptionally perfumed wine, delivering heavenly aromas of cedar and cassis and spices. It is rich and sleek, plumped up by the Merlot, yet always elegant, and with age it develops a velvety softness. The wine can often be enjoyed young, even in outstanding vintages, but because it is exceptionally well balanced it has the capacity to age for decades.

CHÂTEAU PICHON-LALANDE
Area under vine: 75 hectares
Grape varieties: 45% Cabernet Sauvignon,
35% Merlot, 12% Cabernet Franc,
8% Petit Verdot
Average age of vines: 35 years
Technical director: Thomas Dô-Chi-Nam
Maître de chai: Jean-Michel Estrade
Chef de culture: Michel Gaudet
Oak ageing: 18-22 months in 50% new oak
Second wine: Réserve de la Comtesse
Third wine: Domaine des Gartieux
Average production: 30,000 cases

OPPOSITE: *The garden facade of Château Pichon-Lalande*

Château Longueville au Baron de Pichon-Longueville

CHÂTEAU LONGUEVILLE AU BARON DE PICHON-LONGUEVILLE

Since Châteaux Pichon-Lalande and Pichon-Longueville face each other, separated only by the road to Saint Julien, it is not surprising that a certain rivalry should have developed between the two properties. For many decades until the mid-1980s, there was no contest between the wines of these two estates: those from Pichon-Lalande were invariably superior to that of its neighbour. In the 1990s, thanks to huge investments in Pichon-Longueville along with a firm commitment to higher quality, the issue is no longer so clear-cut, and the rivalry has, if anything, intensified.

It will be recalled in the preceeding chapter that in 1850, on the death of Joseph de Pichon-Longueville, the two Pichon estates were divided among his four surviving children. His son Raoul inherited what is now Château Pichon-Longueville. After his death, in 1860, his share of the estate passed to a cousin, also named Raoul. The château and vineyards continued to be passed down through the family line until 1933, when the last member of the family sold the estate to the Bouteiller family.

It was Jean Bouteiller who managed the property until his death in 1961. Jean's son Bertrand inherited the estate, but because he was young and inexperienced he placed the running of Pichon in the hands of cellarmasters who were unable to maintain the quality of the wine. There was clearly insufficient investment too, as the 14 shareholders were each keen to maintain their share of the profits.

By the 1970s the reputation of the wine had sunk. It should be noted that Pichon-Longueville was placed above Pichon-Lalande in the 1855 *classement*, and insiders familiar with every hectare of Pauillac are almost unanimous in maintaining that, when it came to acquiring the top vineyards, Raoul got the better bargain in 1850. This was certainly not reflected in the wines of the 1960s and 1970s, when no one could doubt that Pichon Lalande's wines were immensely superior, especially in perfume and finesse. The wines of Pichon Longueville's had become burly and coarse, not lacking in fruit, but over-extracted and without much subtlety.

By the late 1980s the Bouteiller family had run out of steam and agreed to sell the estate. The purchaser was AXA Millésimes, the wine subsidiary of the vast French insurance company AXA. Jean-Michel Cazes of Château Lynch-Bages was already associated with AXA Millésimes through their joint company Châteaux et Associés. Pichon-Longueville is now administered by Châteaux et Associés, with Monsieur Cazes and his very able winemaker and technical director Daniel Llose responsible for the estate and its wines.

The property AXA placed in their hands was in poor condition. The vineyards in production had dwindled to 33 hectares, and the *chais* were run down. The château itself, which had been designed by Charles Burguet in 1851, was sound in structure but had an interior in urgent need of repair and decoration. AXA Millésimes paid 200 million francs for the estate, a further 80 million for the stock, and then spent large sums on renovation and the new *chais*.

Fortunately there was ample room for expansion. Near Batailley and close to the spot where Pauillac meets the Haut-Médoc, a large fallow vineyard called Sainte Anne was acquired, and other vineyards were purchased in various parts of Pauillac. This more than doubled the area under vine to 68 hectares.

The château, an imposing Renaissance-style mansion with spiky corner turrets, was thoroughly restored and furnished in an appropriate mid-nineteenth-century style. It is not inhabited – nor had it been by the Bouteillers, which in large part explains why it was in such shabby condition by 1987 – but has been fitted up with guest rooms, salons, and a billiard room.

The château is of minor interest compared to what has been done to the *chais*. AXA decided to start from scratch and commission new *chais*. They organized an architectural competition, and it is fascinating to see the various designs that were proposed (the mock-ups are on display at the winery). The challenge was not simply to design an efficient modern winemaking facility, it also had to harmonize with the surrounding landscape and with the nineteenth-century château. The winning architects were the Franco-American team of Patrick Dillon and Jean de Gastines. The design, at least the exterior, takes some getting used to, but the more familiar I become with it the more triumphant it seems to be.

Approached down the D2 from Pauillac, you pass between high concrete walls, with a baroque flourish topping each side. It looks rather brutal, though at night when the curlicues are illuminated the effect is dramatic, giving the impression of driving through a triumphal gateway.

The buildings are divided into two sections, a *cuvier* and the *chais à barriques*. They are separated by a shallow fish pool placed in front of the château. Because the buildings are sunk into the ground, they are unobtrusive and blend harmoniously into the landscape. They are decoratively low-key, with mere inverted triangles for windows and just the occasional stone flourish to impart vigour and flair to the design.

A visitors' reception centre has been provided which includes a small boutique where some of the wines are offered for sale. Visitors can tour the winery, and one of the clever aspects of the design is that walkways

have been provided so that visitors can saunter through the whole winery without disturbing those at work within it. The *cuvier* is circular, with leaning columns supporting a central dome. Each stainless-steel tank is fully computerized and the *maître de chai* can obtain a complete history of the vinification. The Cazes team find this technology most helpful when putting together the final blends.

The vineyards are planted with 70 percent Cabernet Sauvignon, and a sizable proportion of Merlot, some 25 percent. The average age of the vines is 30 years and they are planted to a density of about 9,000 vines per hectare. In 1983 Pichon-Longueville began to harvest by machine, but as soon as Jean-Michel Cazes took control of the running of the estate he discontinued the practice. He also introduced *triage à la vigne*.

Until the new *cuvier* came into operation in 1991, the must was fermented in cement, epoxy-resin-lined tanks, which were first installed in the 1960s. Today, all the vinification takes place in temperature-controlled steel tanks. The *marc* is pressed in gentle pneumatic presses and the wine is aged in *barriques* for 12 to 15 months. After AXA took over, half the wine was aged in new oak, but in subsequent vintages the proportion has been increased. The *élevage* is conducted on much the same lines as those found at Château Lynch-Bages.

Everyone noted the excellence of the 1986 vintage. But Cazes and Llose had not made this wine since their responsibility for vinification did not begin until 1987. However, they were responsible for the *élevage* and introduced changes which made an immediate impact on the quality of the wine. They eliminated pumping during racking and protected the wine from

Château Pichon-Longueville at night

oxidation by the use of nitrogen blankets. The result is a wine far fresher and more vigorous than preceding vintages.

Despite its proximity to Château Pichon-Lalande and Saint Julien, the wine here is very different from both. It is a robust, full-throated Pauillac, bold and highly flavoured. It does not have the perfume and delicacy of Pichon-Lalande, in part because it has a much higher proportion of Cabernet Sauvignon in the blend. Comparisons with Lynch-Bages are inevitable, especially as there is widespread agreement that Lynch-Bages has been producing wines of second-growth quality for some years.

Although the winemaking philosophy behind both wines is almost identical, Pichon-Longueville seems to have an edge in elegance, while Lynch-Bages has, initially, richer, bolder flavours. The improvement in the quality of the wine since the sale to AXA Millésimes was almost instantaneous and the true character of this great estate has been restored.

In the 1980s everyone knew that the wines of Pichon-Longueville were completely overshadowed by those of its neighbour, Pichon-Lalande. When the property was sold, I doubt that many people foretold the speed with which the estate would be resurrected and returned to its rightful place as one of the very top wines of Pauillac following the first growths. Although much credit must be given to the Cazes team, no doubt amply assisted by the vast financial resources of AXA, it is also a triumph of *terroir*. Great wine cannot be made by technology alone.

CHÂTEAU PICHON-LONGUEVILLE
Area under vine: 68 hectares
Grape varieties: 70% Cabernet Sauvignon, 25% Merlot, 5% Cabernet Franc
Average age of vines: 30 years
Administrator: Jean-Michel Cazes
Director: Daniel Llose
Technical director: Jean-René Matignon
Maître de chai: Patrick Pinto
Oak ageing: 12-15 months in 60% new oak
Second wine: Les Tourelles de Longueville
Average production: 25,000 cases (plus 10,000 cases Les Tourelles)

The new chai at Pichon-Longueville

A stainless-steel tank, Château Lynch-Bages

The Fourth and Fifth Growths

❧

CHÂTEAUX

Duhart-Milon-Rothschild • D'Armailhac • Batailley • Clerc-Milon • Croizet-Bages

Grand-Puy-Ducasse • Grand-Puy-Lacoste • Haut-Bages-Libéral • Haut-Batailley

Lynch-Bages • Lynch-Moussas • Pédesclaux • Pontet-Canet

The vineyards of Château Batailley in spring

There is just one fourth growth in Pauillac, Duhart-Milon-Rothschild.

The twelve fifth growths are considered in this chapter in alphabetical order.

❧

CHÂTEAU DUHART-MILON-ROTHSCHILD

In the early eighteenth century, Duhart-Milon was a large estate and had a good reputation, though not much is known about Monsieur Duhart, its original owner. In the 1830s the owner was a Monsieur Mandavi, but after his death the property came into the hands of Pierre Castéja. The Castéjas have long been a prominent Médocain family, both as *négociants* and as the owners of Châteaux Batailley and Lynch-Moussas in Pauillac, Château Beau-Site in Saint Estèphe, and Château Doisy-Védrines in Barsac.

Duhart-Milon remained in the hands of the Castéja family until the late 1930s, when it was sold for the relatively trifling sum of 400,000 francs. In the 1920s the *régisseur* was Alain Delon, whose grandson Michel is the proprietor of Château Léoville-Las Cases. It appears that the estate was financially undernourished and 15 hectares of its vineyards were sold off in the 1930s to Château Batailley. During and immediately after World War II Duhart-Milon changed hands many times, and the vineyards suffered from neglect, with many missing vines. A mere 17 hectares remained in production.

Duhart-Milon was bought by the Domaines Barons de Rothschild in 1962, and in 1995 the Chalone Wine Group of California acquired a 24-percent interest in the property. What the Rothschilds found in the vineyard must have convinced them that it was a hopeless case, and they grubbed up all the vines and replanted them and installed proper drainage systems. The vineyards lie about one kilometre southwest of the Rothschilds' beloved Château Lafite.

Duhart-Milon's original seventeenth-century château, along the quay, was torn down and replaced in 1962 by a long, modern-looking house, now the home of André Cazes, the former mayor of Pauillac. The *chais* are in the midst of the town of Pauillac. In 1974 the wooden vats in the *cuvier* were replaced by enamel-lined tanks, and more recently stainless-steel tanks have been added.

The vineyards are managed and the wines are made by the same team responsible for Lafite. The same principles of viticulture are observed at both. Although Duhart-Milon, now that its 30-year-old vines are maturing, produces a fine and well-structured wine, it bears little resemblance to its distinguished neighbour. The grapes tend to ripen about a week later than Lafite's, which is not so much a reflection of the backwardness of the more inland Duhart-Milon vineyards as a confirmation of the precocity of Lafite's superb sites. The Duhart vineyards, essentially a single large parcel, are also flatter than Lafite's and have less exceptional exposure, especially since they are slightly tilted towards the north. Nor is the quality of gravel as superlative as it is at Lafite.

Nonetheless Charles Chevallier and the rest of his team give the same scrupulous attention to Duhart-Milon that they lavish on Lafite. Cabernet Sauvignon is the dominant variety, and there is about 26 percent of Merlot. Merlot is a much more important component of the second wine, Moulin de Duhart, introduced in 1986. As the vines continue to mature, it is likely that the proportion released as the second wine will diminish.

The *cuvier* in Pauillac is very functional, but the *chai*, at 110 metres in length, is the longest in the Médoc. The Domaines Barons de Rothschild are planning to construct a tasting room and reception hall at Duhart to help give the estate an identity of its own. Since it lacks a château and is also linked closely in the minds of the wine trade with Lafite (a connection assisted by the similarity in style of the labels of the two wines), Duhart has always lacked an image of its own.

It certainly has quite a strong character, though one far removed from the elegance of Lafite. Duhart-Milon is a dark tannic wine built for long ageing. What it lacks in initial charm it makes up for in density, and recent vintages, made from more mature vines, have had powerful concentration. Its former earthiness is also diminishing now that the vineyards are older. Despite the structured nature of the wine, Chevallier and his team have been careful not to subject it to excessive doses of new oak. Until 1995 the proportion of new oak has been one-third, but with the excellent 1996 vintage the proportion was increased to 50 percent. Whether this will prove to be a precedent is too early to say.

CHÂTEAU DUHART-MILON-ROTHSCHILD
Area under vine: 67 hectares
Grape varieties: 71% Cabernet Sauvignon, 26% Merlot, 3% Cabernet Franc
Average age of vines: 30 years
General director: Charles Chevallier
Maître de chai: Francis Huguet
Chef de culture: Alain Bossuet
Oak ageing: 15 months in 35-50% new oak
Second wine: Moulin de Duhart
Average production: 18,500 cases

❧

CHÂTEAU D'ARMAILHAC

The history of this estate is exceedingly, needlessly, complicated, especially in the twentieth century, when its name was constantly changed. It was a rich bourgeois, Dominique d'Armailhacq, who developed the estate during the second quarter of the eighteenth century, gradually expanding its vineyards. He also acquired the existing château at what was then Château Brane-Mouton, enabling him to name his property Château Mouton-d'Armailhacq.

The obscurity of the wine, which was never as celebrated as its neighbour Brane-Mouton, did not prevent Dominique's descendants from expanding the property by acquiring some land on the famous Carruades in 1838. In 1843 the owner, Joseph Odet d'Armailhacq, was in debt as a consequence of tariff barriers hampering the export of Bordeaux wines.

Château d'Armailhac

He was forced to sell the estate, but it was acquired the following year by his ex-wife, who financed the purchase by selling the then unplanted Carruades site to Château Lafite.

Her son, Armand d'Armailhacq, born in 1798, achieved lasting fame as the author of an excellent book on Bordeaux, *La Culture des Vignes dans le Médoc*. Despite the sale of the Carruades sector, he was able to expand the estate, and by the time of the 1855 classification an impressive 63 hectares were flourishing. After his death, the estate passed to his brother-in-law, Comte Adrien de Ferrand, whose descendants continued to own d'Armailhacq until its sale by Comte Roger de Ferrand to the Baron Philippe de Rothschild in 1933.

Baron Philippe allowed the elderly Comte Roger to remain in the château for the rest of his life, and as part of that generous offer, he acquired not only the vineyards but the flagging *négociant* business, the Société Vinicole de Pauillac, founded by the comte in 1922. This gave the baron a vehicle for his own *négociant* enterprise, La Baronnie, now known as Baron Philippe de Rothschild S.A. What must also have pleased Baron Philippe is that he had, at last, a decent park adjacent to Mouton.

The chai at d'Armailhac

CHÂTEAU D'ARMAILHAC
Area under vine: 50 hectares
Grape varieties: 55% Cabernet Sauvignon,
20% Merlot, 25% Cabernet Franc
Average age of vines: 35 years
Directors: Patrick Léon and Hervé Berland
Winemaker: Patrick Léon
Maître de chai: Eric Tourbier
Chef de culture: Gilles Rey
Oak ageing: 16 months in 30% new oak
Average production: 21,000 cases

The château at Armailhacq was less enticing and remains incomplete. Built in the 1820s, the plans were overly ambitious and there was never enough money to complete it, which explains its bizarre appearance.

Having acquired the property, Baron Philippe resisted the temptation to incorporate it into the Mouton-Rothschild estate, which might have diminished the quality of the first growth's wines, and changed its name to Château Mouton-Baron-Philippe, as he was entitled to do as the new proprietor. Initially, many of the vineyards were leased to Château Pontet-Canet, but that arrangement ceased shortly before World War II. Baron Philippe set about renovating the property and replanting the vineyards.

At one time the third largest estate in Pauillac, Mouton-d'Armailhacq had diminished to 60 hectares in the 1930s. Baron Philippe could not afford to replant the whole vineyard area, so the area under vine fell to 32 hectares, until in the 1960s the area under vine began once again to climb.

Today the château, which is not inhabited, forms the head of the court-yard, flanked by the *chais* and by offices. Camellia bushes flower against the walls. Part of the *chais* has been converted into a reception hall, lined with the coats of arms and insignia of the leading Bordeaux *négociant* houses. The vineyards needed a lot of work.

The baron wanted to change the name of the estate a second time after the death of his beloved wife Pauline in 1976. He proposed the name of Château Baronne-Pauline, but permission was denied; instead a slight gender change was allowed, and the wine was thereafter labelled Château Mouton-Baronne-Philippe. After the death of Baron Philippe, his daughter Philippine changed the name yet again, releasing the 1991 vintage as Château d'Armailhac, having simplified the spelling of the old name by deleting the 'q'. Her reason for the change was to avoid giving the impression that this was the second wine of Mouton-Rothschild, which at the time had no second wine at all.

About half the vineyards lie just south of the château, between the park and Château Pontet-Canet; the remainder lie to the west of the château and are bordered by those of Mouton-Rothschild. At present about 50 hectares are in production but a further six hectares are being planted. Cabernet Sauvignon plays a far less important role here than at Mouton, but there is a sizable proportion of Cabernet Franc. Some blocks of vines are about a century old. The Mouton team are responsible for the viticulture and winemaking at d'Armailhac.

As at Mouton, the must is fermented at a fairly high temperature, up to 32 degrees Centigrade, and blended soon after the malolactic fermentation is completed. The wine is then transferred to *barriques* and aged, ever since the 1985 vintage, for some 16 months. About one-third of the barrels are new and the remainder are casks that were used to age the previous vintage at Mouton. The wines are then fined with eggwhite and given a rough filtration before bottling in June.

As a wine, d'Armailhac has a different character both to Mouton-Rothschild and Clerc-Milon. The latter two are distinctly Pauillac because of their strong Cabernet Sauvignon character. D'Armailhac, with its large proportions of Merlot and Cabernet Franc, is softer, more delicate, less structured. It is graceful rather than powerful, medium-bodied rather than full and dense. In tastings alongside the other two wines from the Baron Philippe stable it tends to show less impressively, but it is nevertheless a superior wine in its own right. It is perplexing, given the excellent location of its vineyards close both to Mouton and to Pontet-Canet, that the wines are not firmer and more robust, but no doubt the grape variety blend plays an important part in determining their character and structure.

A harvester sorts the grapes

CHÂTEAU BATAILLEY

The vineyards of Batailley lie some way inland in the southern half of Pauillac. It is possible that the estate derives its name from the word *bataille* after a battle which pitched French forces against retreating English troops following the decisive encounter at Castillon in 1483. The vineyards were established by the end of the eighteenth century, when the then owners, two sisters named Saint-Martin, sold the estate in 1791 to a wine merchant called Jean-Guillaume Pécholier. On his death the property passed to his son-in-law, an admiral named de Bédout. In 1816 the admiral died and the estate was sold at auction. The purchaser was the Bordeaux *négociant* Daniel Guestier.

Guestier expanded the vineyards, and Batailley remained in his family until 1866, when it was sold to another of the Parisian bankers who was to make an impact on Pauillac. This was Constant Halphen, and he paid 500,000 francs for the estate, which then consisted of 55 hectares. In 1932, Batailley returned to the hands of a *négociant* family, when the Halphens sold the property to Marcel and François Borie. During World War II the Bories decided to divide Batailley, which is how Château Haut-Batailley came into existence. Marcel kept the château of Batailley and the major portion of the vineyard, while François took the smaller portion, which was subsequently united with a 15-hectare parcel acquired from the then run-down Duhart-Milon vineyards.

After the death of Marcel Borie, in 1961, Batailley was inherited by his daughter Denise, who had married Émile Castéja, the managing director of the respected *négociant* house of Borie-Manoux. The Castéjas had been the proprietors of Duhart-Milon and other properties in the Médoc, and succeeding members of the family had been prominent in the legal profession through the nineteenth century.

Émile and Denise Castéja live at the château, a stocky building, enlarged with pavilions and wings to form an E-shaped structure enclosing a courtyard dominated by an immense pine. Lions adorn the gateposts. The main entrance used to be on what is now the garden side of the building and is the view that still appears on the label of the wine.

Little of the interior has been altered in a century. There is sombre wood panelling in many rooms, and a small but lofty library crammed with ledgers, leather-bound sets, and Monsieur Castéja's impressive collection of books about wine, especially the wines of Bordeaux. A decayed map of 1845 hanging in a side room shows in immense detail the precise ownership of the vineyards at that time. Behind the château lies a beautiful large park with many noble trees laid out by the landscape gardener often employed by Napoleon III.

Émile Castéja is a magisterial figure, immensely knowledgeable about the history of the Médoc; his wife Denise is every bit as informed. Visitors fortunate enough to encounter the Castéjas can enjoy a journey back into the history of the region.

The vineyards are situated on the opposite side of the road that separates Batailley from Lynch-Moussas. The soil is relatively homogeneous and higher than it looks, with some slopes

Château Batailley

rising to about 25 metres. This part of the plateau is a deep gravel bed lying on a base of clay and sandstone. Cabernet Sauvignon dominates the vineyards, though Émile Castéja points out that the *encépagement* in the vineyard does not always reflect the blend of varieties in the finished wine.

The *chai* at Batailley is quite striking. Long, beamed, and low, with iron candelbra casting a dim light onto the lines of barrels, it dates from the 1840s but has been altered. Part of the *chai* was the former *cuvier*. In the late nineteenth century the area between the two principal *chais* was roofed over, creating a handsome shed with a spirited ironwork roof. Attached to the second-year *chai à barriques,* slightly below ground level, are *cuviers,* added on in 1967 and 1980. Four *foudres* stand at the ends of rows of stainless-steel tanks, just for show!

The distinguished oenologist, Professor Pascal Ribereau-Gayon of the University of Bordeaux, is the consultant to the estate, which is now making a consistent style of wine. The *cuvaison,* often around 15 days, is shorter than that at many other estates. Nonetheless the wine is aged for some 18 months in 50 percent new oak. Perhaps the short maceration period contributes to the fairly easygoing style of the wine, which is not always among the most long-lived of Pauillacs. The distribution system here is slightly unusual as there is an exclusivity arrangement with the family firm of Borie-Manoux. The wine is reasonably priced, which, ironically, may contribute to its lack of reputation among avid wine collectors.

Some knowledgeable members of the Bordeaux wine trade have suggested that the relative lightness of Batailley may also result from a lack of selection, although there is a second

The chai at Batailley

Émile Castéja in his study at Château Batailley

wine. 'The Castéjas,' said one insider, 'are still essentially merchants and like to make as much *grand vin* as they can hope to sell. Old-fashioned families such as this are being left behind, as their neighbours pull out all the stops in their search for quality.' Nonetheless, Émile Castéja insists that the reason he made a good, very palatable wine in a dismal year such as 1992 is because 'we had the courage to reject half the crop.' Batailley is a perplexing wine: charming, fruity, well balanced, finely textured, enjoyable. But it does not often have the depth, concentration, and structure expected from a leading Pauillac, which suggests that yields at Batailly may be on the generous side. Émile Castéja knows as much about the history of the Médoc as anyone in the region, yet his own wine remains a less than inspiring example.

CHÂTEAU BATAILLEY
Area under vine: 52 hectares
Grape varieties: 74% Cabernet Sauvignon, 20% Merlot, 5% Cabernet Franc, 1% Petit Verdot
General director: Émile Castéja
Maître de chai: Olivier Guerin
Chef de culture: Bernard Coureau
Oak ageing: 18 months in 50% new oak
Second wine: Pauillac Borie
Average production: 22,500 cases

Vineyards near Château Clerc-Milon

~

CHÂTEAU CLERC-MILON

For some years Clerc-Milon has been an under-estimated and under-priced wine, but in recent years there has been a growing recognition that the wine made at this estate is of fine and consistent quality. Sadly, it is no longer the great bargain it was in the late 1980s.

This property is the third classified growth acquired by Baron Philippe de Rothschild. It takes its name from Monsieur Clerc, who was the owner when the 1855 *classement* was made. He died in 1863, and the estate was inherited by his widow. It did not remain in his family for long; it was split up in 1877 and sold from proprietor to proprietor until, in the 1960s, it was the property of a local lawyer, Jacques Vialard. At the time it was known as Clerc-Milon-Mondon, as Jacques Mondon had been one of the owners of the portion sold by the widow of Monsieur Clerc. After Vialard's death, in 1970, the estate passed to two sisters, Mademoiselle Marie Vialard and Madame Hedon.

It was from these sisters that Baron Philippe bought the estate for the very low price of one million francs. He could only have been buying on potential rather than achievement. Clerc-Milon at that time had a dim reputation and only 10.5 hectares were in production, and even they were in poor condition.

Pruning of the vines in winter

Given this situation, one wonders why Baron Philippe was interested in this dilapidated estate. It was surely the excellent soils of the remaining vineyards, and his acute sense of the potential of the property – one that has been splendidly realised over the past decade. Shortly before the sale, Mademoiselle Vialard had sold off many of the vineyard parcels formerly belonging to Château Clerc-Milon, so the baron bought them back to reconstitute the estate.

Milon is a hamlet just west of Château Lafite, but most of the estate's vines lie near Mousset, a hamlet just north of Le Pouyalet. It is a preposterously fragmented property, with over 100 parcels of vines. The *cuvier* was located next to an unassuming house near the vineyards and a dozen other spaces were rented. However, this was clearly impractical, and in the 1990s new custom-made *chais* were constructed in Pauillac at the northern end of the quay.

The soils are very varied. Closer to the river there is a clay subsoil, but the vines near Milon have sand mixed with the gravel. The grapes mature relatively late. The must is fermented principally in stainless-steel tanks, though a few cement tanks are still in use. The fermentation takes about eight days, and then there is a lengthy maceration period, giving that long *cuvaison* typical of the Mouton group of properties. The malolactic fermentation takes place in the tanks, the wine is usually blended in November, then goes into barrels for its *élevage* of 16 to 18 months in 30 percent new oak. Some of the older barrels come from Mouton, where they have been previously used for a single wine. There is an eggwhite fining and a rough filtration before the wine is bottled.

If tastings of Château d'Armailhac leave slight feelings of disappointment, the same cannot be said of Château Clerc-Milon. Baron Philippe's instincts proved sound, and the wine goes from strength to strength. It is a distinguished Pauillac, elegant with deep colour, rich meaty aroma, and depth of flavour and longevity on the palate. It appears that the Rothschild sales team are well aware that Clerc-Milon has been a bargain, and it seems likely that *en primeur* prices are set to rise.

CHÂTEAU CLERC-MILON
Area under vine: 30 hectares
Grape varieties: 70% Cabernet Sauvignon, 20% Merlot, 10% Cabernet Franc
Average age of vines: 40 years
Directors: Patrick Léon and Hervé Berland
Winemaker: Patrick Léon
Maître de chai: Eric Tourbier
Chef de culture: Gilles Rey
Oak ageing: 16-18 months in 30% new oak
Average production: 15,000 cases

CHÂTEAU CROIZET-BAGES

There is no intrinsic reason why Croizet-Bages should not be a very good and dependable wine. The vines lie on the Bages plateau in a single parcel that touches the vineyards of Grand-Puy-Lacoste, Grand-Puy-Ducasse, and Batailley, as well as Lynch-Bages, its most celebrated neighbour. The gravel is not especially deep here, but below it lies a band of red sand which retains water, and below that a deeper band of white sand with large stones that offers good drainage, making drought problems a rarity. The vineyard is well ventilated and there is often a fresh wind blowing across its expanses.

Part of the problem at Croizet-Bages may derive from factors beyond the immediate control of the owner. Much of the vineyard was replanted in the 1980s, and some of the root-stocks chosen have proved far from ideal. The density of plantation is about 6,500 vines per hectare. Some vines are at least 50 years old and the new director is anxious to preserve them.

The estate is named after the two brothers who created it in the eighteenth century. Early in the following century they sold it to Jean de Puytarec, who kept it until 1853, when he sold it to Julien Calvé. Calvé built himself a mansion along the quayside at Pauillac and used its image on the label of his wine, although the château is no longer part of the property. In 1934 the Calvé family sold the estate to Paul Quié, whose son Jean-Michel inherited the property on Paul's death in 1968. The Quiés also own Château Rauzan-Gassies in Margaux

Architectural detail, Château Croizet-Bages

(another under-achiever) and the Haut-Médoc property of Château Bel-Orme Tronquoy-de-Lalande.

Paul Quié, who lives with his family in Paris, made his fortune as a *négociant* in northern France, enabling him to buy these three estates when prices were extremely low. No doubt the family business supplied ample markets for this Pauillac, so there may have been little incentive to produce a wine of real quality. But this is speculation. What is clear is that in the 1990s someone came to the belated realisation that Croizet-Bages was slipping ever further behind its ambitious neighbours in Pauillac and decided to do something about it.

A new director has been installed at the Quié properties: Jean-Louis Camp. This burly, rather shy but nonetheless communicative man has had long experience in the region, and worked for many years at the well-known property of Château Loudenne. He is too discreet to say so, but it seems clear that he well understands the shortcomings of Croizet-Bages and is keen to ameliorate the situation. He seems none too happy with the high percentage of Merlot in the vineyard and would like to plant more Cabernet Sauvignon. Some decades ago the proportion of Cabernet was far higher at Croizet-Bages, and I have not yet discovered when it was lowered to its current 50 percent. Camp would like to have at least 60 percent in the vineyards, which would give the wine more backbone.

Merlot juice being drained from steel tanks at Croizet-Bages

The soil is relatively productive, but Croizet-Bages seems untroubled by high yields, even though there are years in which even this estate feels compelled to green-harvest. There are in effect two harvests from the vineyards. The young vines are picked first, by hand, removing the bunches that are not destined for the *grand vin,* either because of their youth or because of any maladies. The rest of the crop is picked by machine, a rarity among classified growths in Pauillac. Whatever the merits or demerits of mechanical harvesting, Camp says that only healthy and mature grapes end up in the fermentation vats.

The old *cuvier* at Croizet-Bages, with its wooden vats, is no longer in use and now functions as a kind of museum. The must is fermented in stainless-steel tanks that were installed in the late 1980s. Camp believes in bleeding the tanks to increase concentration, and usually eliminates up to 15 percent of the must in this way. Enzymes are added to aid colour extraction, then yeasts are inoculated and the must heated to provoke the fermentation. Camp likes to ferment at temperatures up to 31 degrees Centigrade, with ample pumping over. A peculiarity of the vinification here is that in certain vintages the wine is briefly heated up to 55 degrees Centigrade at the very end of the *cuvaison.* Not surprisingly this gives considerably greater extraction and, according to Camp, precludes the

CHÂTEAU CROIZET-BAGES
Area under vine: 30 hectares
Grape varieties: 50% Cabernet Sauvignon, 40% Merlot,
10% Cabernet Franc
Average age of vines: 30 years
Director: Jean-Louis Camp
Maître de chai: Philippe Dorbessan
Oak ageing: 12-16 months in 15% new oak
Average production: 11,500 cases

need to add press wine to the blend. Nevertheless, Camp is careful not to submit more than about 15 percent of the wine to this treatment. He acknowledges that this technique can produce rather cooked wines unless it is very carefully monitored.

Until 1994 there was no new oak used for the *élevage* of Croizet-Bages. Jean-Louis Camp has now introduced between 10 and 15 percent of new oak barrels. He also points out that the oldest barrels in use are only five years old, which gives rise to the question of how old they were before Camp took over. Camp admits he is not an enthusiast for new oak, and given the lack of concentration in most vintages at Croizet-Bages, this is just as well. He is quite keen on the attributes of American oak, but I have the impression that not a great deal is used here. Until recently unsatisfactory lots were sold off to wholesalers, but Camp is now planning to introduce a second wine.

Croizet-Bages has come in for some richly deserved brickbats from most of those who have written about its wine. Until Monsieur Camp's arrival there was no serious attempt to make a wine worthy of its status. Considering what has been achieved, almost every year, at its neighbours Lynch-Bages and Grand Puy Lacoste, the mediocrity of Croizet-Bages has been little short of a disgrace. However, the arrival of Jean-Louis Camp augurs well.

A cluster of Cabernet Franc

CHÂTEAU GRAND-PUY-DUCASSE

Both Grand-Puy-Ducasse and Grand-Puy-Lacoste derive their names from Grand Puy, the name given to a plateau that lies in the western part of Pauillac. *Puy*, like *fite* and *motte*, means a mound, and thus was another act of homage to a gentle gravel slope. However, not all the vineyards of Grand-Puy-Ducasse, as it is constituted today, lie on the Grand Puy itself. Its three main parcels are between Mouton-Rothschild and Pontet-Canet; another borders Batailley and Lynch-Moussas; and the smallest parcel lies between Lynch-Bages and Grand-Puy-Lacoste.

The estate takes its name from a family whose founding member in Pauillac was Arnaud Ducasse in the late seventeenth century. He owned a few hectares of vines, supplemented by vineyards brought into the family by his wife near the village of Artigues on the western edge of

Pauillac. The estate remained in the hands of Arnaud's descendants, who gradually expanded the area under vine. It was his son Pierre who acquired land on the Grand Puy from the descendants of Bertrand Dejean, and by means of exchanges concentrated his holdings in this part of the commune, thus forming a property that bears some resemblance to the present-day *cru*. By the end of the eighteenth century the estate was quite sizeable, with some 40 hectares of vines in production.

Arnaud Ducasse built a modest house overlooking the Gironde at Pauillac, but it was one of his descendants, another Pierre Ducasse, who built the château that stands in its place today. Built in the 1820s, it has recently been scrubbed and renovated and makes a handsome neoclassical contribution to the Pauillac waterfront. It used to be the headquarters of the local *confrerie,* the Commanderie du Bontemps.

Pierre Ducasse had two daughters, who died young, yet the property, which had for some time rejoiced in the cumbersome name of Ducasse-Grand-Puy-Artigues-Arnaud, remained intact. In 1855 it was listed as Château Artigues-Arnaud, a name now used for the second wine. Sons-in-law of Pierre enjoyed the succession to the property, one of them being Baron de Suduiraut, whose family remained shareholders until 1971. In the 1860s Grand-Puy-Ducasse was a fragmented property of just under 40 hectares. The estate was financially restructured in 1932, with the Boutellier family of Château Pichon-Longueville becoming the principal shareholders.

The property, however, was allowed to decline. By 1949 it consisted of no more than 10 hectares of vineyards. It was bought by the firm of Mestrezat, in 1971, and these new owners resuscitated this severely neglected property. Mestrezat is a company of Swiss origin with a number of properties in the Bordeaux area, including Château Rayne-Vigneau in Sauternes.

Mestrezat's first task was to restore the vineyards. New plantings were made at a density of 10,000 vines per hectare. In addition, about 20 hectares were purchased, increasing the vineyard area to 36 hectares. That took much of the 1970s, and during the following decade the agricultural buildings next to the château were converted into a *cuvier* and reception hall. Stainless-steel tanks were installed in 1986, replacing the cement tanks previously used. In the late 1990s the *chai à barriques* underwent extensive renovation.

Grand-Puy-Ducasse has not been an outstanding growth under Mestrezat's stewardship, but, as at Croizet-Bages, there has been belated recognition that the estate has been lacklustre for some time. In 1991,

Château Grand-Puy-Ducasse in the town of Pauillac

mechanical harvesting was abandoned and the estate resumed manual picking. Then a sorting table was sent into the vineyards during the harvest to permit *triage* among the vines. The *cuvaison* now extends for at least three weeks at temperatures of up to 32 degrees Centigrade. Malolactic fermentation takes place in tanks, and then the wine is aged for 16 months in *barriques,* of which one-third are new. Grand-Puy-Ducasse relies heavily on the excellent barrels of Séguin-Moreau, supplemented by Taransaud and Sylvain. Bernard Monteau, the estate's oenologist, prefers barrels with a medium toast. The estate fines its wines not with traditional eggwhites, but with albumen, doing so in tanks rather than barrels, and then filters before bottling.

Another indication of the estate's commitment to improved quality is the greater degree of selection. About 60 percent of the wine is chosen for the *grand vin*. The second wine, Artigues-Arnaud, is aged in older barrels. More recently, however, the team introduced a second wine of superior quality called Les Preludes à Grand-Puy-Ducasse.

It is difficult to know what to make of Grand-Puy-Ducasse. There is the potential here for very good wine and there is also reason to believe in Bernard Monteau's commitment to improving quality.

CHÂTEAU GRAND-PUY-DUCASSE
Area under vine: 37 hectares
Grape varieties: 62% Cabernet Sauvignon, 38% Merlot
Average age of vines: 25 years
Technical director: Patrice Bandiera
Maître de chai: Yvon Rautureau
Oenologist: Bernard Monteau
Oak ageing: 16 months in 30% new oak
Second wine: Les Preludes à Grand-Puy-Ducasse
Third wine: Artigues-Arnaud
Average production: 11,000 cases, plus 5,000 cases of Artigues-Arnaud

CHÂTEAU GRAND-PUY-LACOSTE

Grand-Puy-Lacoste is a wine one would select to demonstrate what a Pauillac should taste like. It has never been a flashy wine, but for many years it has been dependable, beautifully made, complex and subtle, and exhibiting all the muscular fruitiness of a fine Pauillac.

The plateau of Grand Puy, in the western part of Pauillac, was owned in the 1720s by Bertrand Dejean, who also owned Lynch-Bages during that decade. The property was inherited by his widow, but she sold much of it in 1743. Dejean seems to have sold some of the land to Pierre Ducasse, and other parcels passed down through the generations into the hands of François Lacoste, who married one of Dejean's descendants. Their son Pierre-Frédéric appears to have developed the property into a substantial wine-producing estate, which merited classification in 1855. After the death of Pierre-Frédéric in 1868, his daughter, the Comtesse de Saint-Léger, inherited the estate. In 1932 the then proprietors, two gentlemen named Hériveau and Néel, sold Grand-Puy-Lacoste to a well-known Bordeaux *bon viveur,* Raymond Dupin.

OPPOSITE: *Château Grand-Puy-Lacoste*

Despite Dupin's passion for the good things of life, he did not seem to have expended much energy on maintaining his vineyards. He preferred to live in Bordeaux, and the property dwindled in size to about 25 hectares, less than half its area during its heyday. Dupin was famous for his lavish meals at the château, cooked by the redoubtable Antoinette, and for the precious old vintages he served with them. However, his generosity did not extend to spending money on his estate, which somehow managed to produce good wine despite his neglect.

In the mid-1970s negotiations began between the ageing bachelor Dupin and the Borie family, who were the owners of Château Ducru-Beaucaillou in Saint Julien. To ease the process of negotiation, the Dupins and Bories would each bring to lunch bottles of their wines from the same vintage. Dupin, François-Xavier Borie tells me, enjoyed these comparative drinking bouts so much that agreement was eventually reached between the two parties. In 1978 the Bories acquired half the shares in Grand-Puy-

Lacoste and took over responsibility for the winemaking. Two years later Raymond Dupin died and the Bories took a majority share of the estate.

Jean-Eugène Borie, whose father had bought Ducru-Beaucaillou in the 1940s, still lives at that delightful château, while his son François-Xavier, born in 1953, lives both in Bordeaux and at Grand-Puy-Lacoste. François-Xavier suggests that his was probably the last private family to buy a classified growth in Pauillac; now, the financial power has moved from private individuals to large companies. The Bories have another château in Pauillac, Haut-Batailley, and are major players in the region.

The main part of the château is a fine sturdy building of the 1850s which suffered from vandalization by German soldiers during World War II. Now restored, it is used for receptions, while the family inhabits a cosy side wing that was once the estate's cooperage. Flanking the entrance courtyard is a neoclassical arcade, and the *chais* are arranged around subsidiary courtyards to the side and rear of the château. Behind the house an enclosed courtyard leads into the large, English-style park. It is a lovely setting. Camellias flourish in the courtyard, and in spring daffodils are sprinkled down the slope leading to the long rectangular pool, populated by families of ducks, and lined by rhododendron bushes.

Apart from the pleasure the Borie children derive from playing in a large park in the heart of Pauillac's vineyards, this bower of greenery and water has, for our purposes, an instructive role to play. From the road to Batailley, the Grand Puy plateau looks like a flat gravel bed. It is only at Grand-Puy-Lacoste, where the steep slope from château to park can be seen, that it becomes apparent that the plateau, in Pauillac terms, is quite high and that its slope offers excellent drainage. Away from the coastal vineyards, such as those of Latour, it is difficult to see what distinguishes the *terroir* of Pauillac from that of, say, its far less esteemed neighbours in the Haut-Médoc going towards Saint-Laurent. Here the specificity of Pauillac *terroir* becomes evident.

The vines lie on two *croupes*. One is on the château's north, south, and east sides, running up to the Saint Laurent road; the second lies to the southwest, and adjoins the vineyards of Batailley and Lynch-Moussas, south of the village of Artigues. The deep gravel soil is fairly homogeneous. Many of the vines are planted from east to west to encourage drainage into the Moussas stream. Old drainage channels were discovered when vineyards were replanted; some channels have been restored, others have been replaced.

The vineyards are planted essentially with Cabernet Sauvignon and Merlot (with a dash of Cabernet Franc) to a density of 10,000 vines per

Garden pool at Grand-Puy-Lacoste

The Fourth and Fifth Growths · 125

The chapel at Grand-Puy-Lacoste

CHÂTEAU GRAND-PUY-LACOSTE
Area under vine: 50 hectares
Grape varieties: 70% Cabernet Sauvignon,
25% Merlot, 5% Cabernet Franc
Average age of vines: 38 years
General director: François-Xavier Borie
Maître de chai: Philippe Gouze
Chef de culture: Marc Duvocelle
Oak ageing: 18 months in 40-50% new oak
Second wine: Lacoste-Borie
Average production: 15,000 cases,
plus 9,000 cases Lacoste-Borie

hectare. When the Bories took over the estate, only 30 hectares were in production, but they also bought the *droit de plantation*, which permitted them to plant a further 20 hectares; an additional 10 remain fallow. This means that there are a number of parcels of young vines, which are used for the second wine, Lacoste-Borie. Fortunately there are also a good number of very old vines, which are replaced individually when they eventually succumb to decrepitude.

François-Xavier Borie considers his vineyards productive, especially the young vines. If the vines are inadvertently pruned too severely, he believes they will compensate the following year, reinforcing their vigour. He will green-harvest if necessary, but only as a last resort. In his experience, at the age of 12 or 15 years the vines tend to find their own natural balance, and then in old age are far less productive and yields cease to be an important issue.

During the harvest there is some initial sorting in the vineyard, and since 1991 there has been a *tapis de triage* at the winery. Also in 1991 stainless-steel tanks were added to the *cuvier*, and Borie is considering replacing the remaining enamel tanks with stainless-steel ones. Borie has tanks of many different sizes allowing him to vinify parcels separately which, in turn, provides a large number of lots for blending. The *cuvaison* lasts up to three weeks. Borie favours a softer extraction and so avoids forceful pumping over or excessively long *cuvaison*. The malolactic fermentation takes place in tanks.

Usually the wine is aged in about 40 percent new oak, but in more structured years such as 1995 and 1996, about 50 percent was used. The estate's principal coopers are Nadalie, Séguin-Moreau, and Taransaud. The *élevage* lasts for 18 months and then the wine is fined with eggwhites. The second wine is mostly a lot selection made in the *cuvier,* but on the other hand the Bories have a shrewd idea about which parcels are likely to provide the weaker wines.

François-Xavier Borie points out that this wine is better known in Britain and the United States than it is in France. If so, this is a cause for Anglophone congratulation. It is a classic Pauillac, with ample cassis fruit, robust structure, and spicy, oaky overtones. One of the very best fifth growths, it would almost certainly be rated higher if a new *classement* were established.

CHÂTEAU HAUT-BAGES-LIBÉRAL

This medium-sized estate, although commercially successful, is not espcially well known. Its early history is obscure, but at the time of the 1855 classification it was owned by a Monsieur Libéral, whose forebears had long been wine brokers in the Bordeaux region and had owned the property since the mid-eighteenth century. The name proved handy, for much of the wine found an enthusiastic market among supporters of Liberal parties in northern Europe.

At the beginning of the twentieth century, the property was sold to the Solminihac family, and thence to various other proprietors who included the Averous and Desse families. It lapsed into obscurity, from which it was rescued in 1960 by a consortium that included the Cruse family of *négociants*. They bought the estate from the Desse family, who were steel-making magnates. The Cruses replanted much of the vineyard but gave some of it to Château Pontet-Canet, of which they were also the proprietors. The wine was initially bottled in Bordeaux, but château-bottling, introduced in the 1970s throughout Bordeaux, obliged the Cruses to modernise the *cuvier* at Haut-Bages-Libéral. From 1960 to 1973 the wine had been vinified at Pontet-Canet.

Despite the investments made by the Cruse family, they sold the property in 1983 to the Bernard Taillan group, who have made a fortune from the branded wine Chantovent. The head of the group was Jacques Merlaut, whose daughter Bernardette, a qualified oenologist

The village of Artigues

Old vines in winter

CHÂTEAU HAUT-BAGES-LIBÉRAL
Area under vine: 28 hectares
Grape varieties: 80% Cabernet Sauvignon,
17% Merlot, 3% Petit Verdot
Average age of vines: 30 years
Director: Alain Sutre
Maître de chai: Daniel Sore
Oak ageing: 14-16 months in 40% new oak
Second wine: La Chapelle de Bages
Average production: 9,000 cases,
plus 6,500 cases La Chapelle de Bages

and one of Bordeaux's few women winemakers, ran the estate together with the well-known *cru bourgeois* Château Chasse-Spleen. She introduced new *barriques*, which were rarely seen in its *chais* during the reign of the Cruses. Bernardette and her husband were killed in a climbing accident in November 1992. For a brief period her brother Jean Merlaut ran the property, but it is now being managed by Bernardette's daughter Claire, and the oenologist Alain Sutre, who looks after many of the Bernard Taillan properties.

There is no real château at Haut-Bages-Libéral. Instead, at the head of the lane leading to the winery, there is a small *maison bourgeoise*. The winery stands on a ridge just east of the village of Saint Lambert and to the north of the Latour vineyards. Although it is tempting to think that Haut-Bages-Libéral must share characteristics with that great first growth, the soil is quite different and the drainage inferior. The *croupe* at Haut-Bages-Libéral lies on a subsoil of clay and limestone, topped with gravel (the larger stones known as *galets*) and sand.

The vineyards share Château Latour's proximity to the Gironde, which protects them from frost. Even in 1991, Haut-Bages-Libéral had yields of 36 hectolitres per hectare. Not all the vines are around the winery. Some are on the Bages plateau; others adjoin those of Pichon-Longueville and Pichon-Lalande, but there are many young vines in this parcel. Vines are planted to a density of 9,000 to 10,000 per hectare, and about two-thirds of the vines are now more than 35 years old. As the vines age they are replaced individually.

The grapes are harvested manually, with *triage* in the vineyard. Yields are high, often, as in 1995, close to the maximum. Claire Villars and Alain Sutre have opted for a very long *cuvaison*, sometimes as long as five weeks, at up to 32 degrees Centigrade. But these are nuances. The aim is slow and gentle extraction.

Although the fermentation takes place in stainless-steel tanks, the château is now doing the malolactic fermentation in *barriques*. I suspect that both the long *cuvaison* and the malolactic in wood are strategies to soften the wine in its youth, as Haut-Bages-Libéral has long had a reputation for being tough, especially when young, which is when crucial commercial judgements are often made. The underlying clay soil undoubtedly contributes to the tannic grip of this wine.

The wine is aged for 14 to 16 months in barrels, of which about 40 percent are new. Before the wine is bottled in April, there is the usual fining and a light filtration. The second wine, La Chapelle de Bages, is a barrel selection, mostly mopping up the young vines. About half the wine produced is now exported.

There is unquestionably fine potential at Haut-Bages-Libéral. While it may never be a wine of finesse, it does show excellent richness as well as muscular fruit and tannin. Claire Villars is married to one of the innumerable members of the Lurton family – her husband Gonzague is the proprietor of Château Dufort-Vivens in Margaux – and between them the Villars and the Lurtons run at least a dozen top Bordeaux estates. They are ambitious, energetic, capable. So there is every reason to expect some notable achievements from Haut-Bages-Libéral in the years to come.

❧

CHÂTEAU HAUT BATAILLEY

In my description of Château Batailley, I explained how the estate came to be divided in the 1940s. The share of the property that went to François Borie was the smaller of the two and lacked a château; it was soon expanded with the acquisition of 15 hectares of vineyards that belonged to Château Duhart-Milon. This newly created domaine was given the name Haut-Batailley. François Borie died in 1953, and his daughter Françoise de Brest-Borie inherited the property. She remains the owner, but has lived for many years in Limoges and takes no part in the daily running of the estate. So she has rented the property to her brother Jean-Eugène, the owner of Château Ducru-Beaucaillou, and in practice it is Jean-Eugène's son François-Xavier who manages the estate, just as he does Grand-Puy-Lacoste.

The estate, by Pauillac standards, is quite small, with 22 hectares in production, although the Bories have the right to plant a further 13 hectares. The nineteenth-century *chais*, built in

Château Haut-Batailley

a style vaguely reminiscent of a Swiss chalet, stand just to the west of Château Batailley. One section of the vineyards lies behind those *chais*, on either side of the railway track; they are close to the famous vineyards of Petit Batailley from which Les Forts de Latour is largely derived. Another section is further north, on the Bages plateau. The soil near the château is quite gravelly, and the vines usually mature later than those on the Bages plateau.

Until 1974 vinification took place at Ducru-Beaucaillou, but that year the *cuvier* was re-equipped with a double tier of tanks: enamel above, cement below. A functional new *chai* was built in 1987 alongside the original structures. The vinification and *élevage* of Haut-Batailley do not differ markedly from those practiced at Grand-Puy-Lacoste, except that a smaller proportion of new oak barrels is used – about one-third – as the wine tends to be less structured. The second wine, La Tour d'Aspic, is a selection made in the winery. In style, Haut-Batailley is often placed in the lighter, more elegant camp, and has often been compared to a Saint Julien. Nonetheless it sometimes strikes me as a burly, old-fashioned wine.

Haut-Batailley often seems to have the components for a very good wine, but they almost never seem to come together harmoniously. Attractive when young, the wines sometimes fall out of balance during their evolution, becoming awkward or dry or occasionally coarse. I rarely detect the elegance that some tasters find in Haut-Batailley. On balance, Batailley seems to be the more satisfying wine. It is perplexing, since the Bories make such wonderfully rich and consistent wine at Grand-Puy-Lacoste and Ducru-Beaucaillou.

CHÂTEAU HAUT-BATAILLEY
Area under vine: 22 hectares
Grape varieties: 65% Cabernet Sauvignon, 25% Merlot, 10% Cabernet Franc
Average age of vines: 30 years
Director: François-Xavier Borie
Maître de chai: René Lusseau
Chef de culture: Francis Souquet
Oak ageing: 14-16 months in 35% new oak
Second wine: Château La Tour d'Aspic
Average production: 10,000 cases

❧

CHÂTEAU LYNCH-BAGES

Lynch is a famous Bordeaux name, originating with an Irish soldier who came to the port and put down roots. But the story of the estate now bearing his name begins earlier. At the beginning of the eighteenth century the owner of the estate that occupied the Bages plateau just outside the town of Pauillac was Bernard Dejean, who also owned the Grand Puy plateau. He sold the property to Pierre Drouillard, who died in 1749. His sister Elisabeth was married to Thomas Lynch, which is how the domaine came into the hands of the Lynch family.

The first of the Bordeaux Lynches was John, an Irish soldier who left Ireland after the defeat at the Battle of the Boyne in 1690. He came to live

OPPOSITE: *Château Lynch-Bages*

A modern bottling machine, Château Lynch-Bages

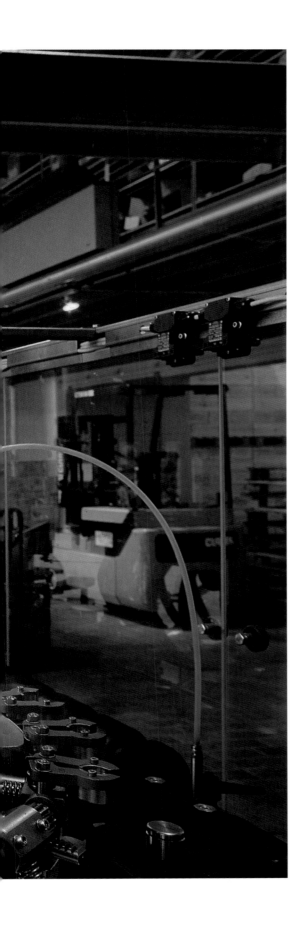

in Bordeaux and he married a Frenchwoman. His sons were brought up in the region and soon prospered. Both Thomas and his nephew Michel managed the estate, while Thomas's son Jean-Baptiste rose to become mayor of Bordeaux in 1749 and was ennobled as a consequence.

Michel Lynch lived to a ripe old age and died in 1841. Seventeen years earlier the estate had been sold to a Swiss merchant named Sébastien Jurine, and Lynch-Bages remained the property of the Jurine family until 1861. It changed owners a few times, passing through the hands of the Cayrou and de Vial families, until in 1939 it was bought by Jean-Charles Cazes. The new owner had been a baker in Pauillac, but when his bakery burnt down in 1924, he switched careers and became an insurance agent and also looked after the vineyards of Château Les-Ormes-de-Pez, the Saint Estèphe property owned by his brother-in-law.

Cazes began managing Lynch-Bages in 1933 and in time knew it well. General Félix de Vial had been an absentee landlord, and during the depressed decade of the 1930s had rented the domaine to Cazes without charge, content to have someone capable looking after the property and trying to make it pay. Cazes must have been a good businessman as well as winemaker, as he found a *négociant* willing to buy the entire crop of the dismal 1933 vintage. By 1939 the general was so strapped for cash that he was only too happy to sell the estate to Cazes, even giving him five years to pay the purchase price. Cazes was by then 62 years old.

Cazes made numerous improvements to the estate and replanted many vines. He died at the age of 95 in 1972, by which time his son André, born in 1913, had been running Lynch-Bages for six years. André Cazes is a well-known and popular figure in the region, having been mayor of Pauillac for 30 years. Although slightly incapacitated by a stroke, he remains a vigorous chronicler of the history of Pauillac, and his appetite for good wine and fine cigars seems undiminished.

Today the estate is run by André's son Jean-Michel, who was born in 1935. He began his working life employed by IBM in Paris and, like his father and grandfather, always maintained a second career as an insurance agent. Soon after the death of his grandfather, Jean-Michel took over the management of the estate as his father, André, had too many other preoccupations, such as administering Pauillac itself. Jean-Michel has greatly expanded the buildings at Lynch-Bages. The nineteenth-century *cuvier* has been restored as a museum showing visitors how wine was made over a hundred years ago.

Excellent wines have been made at Lynch-Bages for many years, but it is Jean-Michel Cazes, and his winemaker Daniel Llose (responsible for Lynch-Bages since 1976), who have ensured that Lynch-Bages remains at

The grounds of Château Lynch-Bages

the forefront of the fifth growths. Among their innovations were the installation of stainless-steel tanks and the use of a far higher proportion of new oak barrels, replacing older casks that could give rise to the risk of volatile acidity and other problems. Few would dispute that were the estates of Pauillac ever to be reclassified, Château Lynch-Bages would be a prime candidate for promotion.

The corporate structure of the estate is complicated but worth explaining. Châteaux Lynch-Bages and Les-Ormes-de-Pez, the latter an excellent *cru bourgeois* in Saint Estèphe, are properties of the Cazes family. However, in 1987 they teamed up with the vast French insurance company AXA to form an umbrella organisation called Châteaux et Associés. Cazes and the founder of AXA, Claude Bébéar, have been friends since their youth and have always enjoyed a relationship of trust. AXA (or, rather, its wine subsidiary AXA Millésimes) owns part of Châteaux et Associés but has no direct stake in the two Cazes properties. However, Châteaux et Associés manages all the estates in the AXA portfolio, which in effect means that Jean-Michel Cazes and Daniel Llose have overall responsibility for the winemaking and administration not only at Lynch-Bages and Les-Ormes-de-Pez, but also at Pichon-Longueville, Petit-Village in Pomerol, Suduiraut in Sauternes, the great port estate of Quinta da Noval in the Douro region of Portugal, and the reborn Tokaj estate of Disznókó in Hungary.

As a consequence, the Cazes family is one of the most internationally minded of all Pauillac proprietors. Travelling incessantly, both to manage the estates and to publicize and promote

The courtyard at Lynch-Bages

their wines, Jean-Michel Cazes understands the demands of markets as disparate as the French, the American, and the Asian. Combining the personalities of *bon viveur* and workaholic, he has a better claim than anyone since Baron Philippe de Rothschild to be a showman and spokesman for the whole region. Some may criticize the lush opulent style of winemaking he and Llose appear to favour, but the results in the bottle are undeniably delicious, full-flavoured, and deservedly popular. Approachable young, the wines also age well.

In 1973 the Cazes family bought the remnants of a *cru bourgeois* called Château Haut-Bages Averous. At first the wine was released as a separate growth, but since 1978 it has been the second wine of Lynch-Bages. It has allowed Cazes to be more severe in his selection. In 1978 only three percent of the Lynch-Bages production went into the second wine; by 1987, a mediocre vintage, it was 35 percent.

Driving south from Pauillac along the D2 in the direction of Bordeaux, Lynch-Bages appears on the right. It's a large estate, dominating the plateau of Bages, capped by the winery buildings from which there are good views of the Gironde estuary. The château, more a comfortable house than a mansion of any pretensions, is believed to have been constructed by Sébastien Jurine in the 1820s.

Most of the vines lie on the Bages plateau between the winery and the D2, and the second plot is not far from Mouton-Rothschild, on both sides of the road from Pauillac to Batailley. Yields are fairly generous, but Llose insists that this is not a case of overcropping. He and his

CHÂTEAU LYNCH-BAGES
Area under vine: 88 hectares
Grape varieties: 73% Cabernet Sauvignon,
15% Merlot, 10% Cabernet Franc,
2% Petit Verdot
Average age of vines: 35 years
Technical director: Daniel Llose
Maître de chai: Guy Bergey
Oak ageing: 12-15 months in 50% new oak
Second wine: Château Haut-Bages-Averous
Average production: 35,000 cases, plus 10,000 cases
Haut-Bages Averous

team take pains to ensure that the vineyards are well maintained and regulated; there are no missing vines, except where vines have been replanted and are not yet in production, and everything is done to ensure that only ripe healthy grapes are harvested. A team of eight sorters sift through the grapes in the vineyard to reject tainted fruit before it has a chance to come into contact with healthy grapes.

Since 1975 the must has been fermented in stainless-steel tanks, and more recently the *évaporation sous-vide* method has been used to concentrate the must if there is any dilution. After a three-week *cuvaison* and the malolactic fermentation, the wine is decanted into *barriques*. Lynch-Bages is always aged in a minimum of 50 percent new oak, and the proportion can increase to 60 percent in outstanding vintages. Cazes and Llose prefer barrels with a medium toast. After ageing the wine for between 12 and 15 months, it is given a very light filtration before bottling in the early summer. The second wine is aged in one-year-old *barriques*.

One curiosity at Lynch-Bages is the presence of white vines. They were planted long ago close to the château, but were not vinified separately until 1978. In 1987 Cazes decided to replant the vineyard with a blend of 40 percent Sauvignon Blanc, 40 percent Semillon, and 20 percent Muscadelle. The first release of the revamped wine, known as Blanc de Lynch-Bages, was in 1990. The style is quite lush and oaky, but not overblown, and about 3,000 cases a year are produced.

Lynch-Bages is a full-throttled Bordeaux, robust but very fruity, a wine often approachable young but capable of very long ageing. It is deeply coloured, cassis-scented, and develops rich cedary flavours with age. It is not the most subtle of great Pauillacs, but is among the most enjoyable.

The tasting room, Château Lynch-Bages

Château Lynch-Moussas

❧

CHÂTEAU LYNCH-MOUSSAS

Château Lynch-Moussas, like Lynch-Bages, takes its name from the Irish Lynch family. It was the property of Comte Jean-Baptiste Lynch, the mayor of Bordeaux, but by the time of the 1855 classification it belonged to the Vasquez family, who were *négociants* specialising in trade with South America. Bought in 1919 by Jean Castéja, the property has remained in the hands of the Castéja family ever since. After Jean's death, in 1955, the property passed to his widow.

The estate remained neglected until Émile Castéja, who is also the owner of Château Batailley, took over the running of the property in 1969. One of Émile Castéja's first projects was to replant almost the entire vineyard. Only eight hectares were in production when he took over Lynch-Moussas. The area now under vine is 54 hectares.

Lynch-Moussas takes the second part of its name from the tiny hamlet of Moussas nearby. The vineyards are in a number of parcels, one close to the château, a second between Grand-Puy-Lacoste and Batailley, a third just to the west of Pichon-Lalande, and a fourth (of five hectares) next to Grand-Puy-Ducasse. The soil resembles that of its partner, Château

An interior view at Lynch-Moussas

Batailley. The château, buried among woods just across the Pauillac boundary, is a stately building with a large courtyard and a good-sized park. It is occasionally inhabited by Émile's son, Philippe Castéja, a well-known Bordeaux *négociant*. The original château was built during the reign of Louis XIII, but the present structure dates from the time of Napoleon III. The old *cuvier* has been transformed into a reception hall and has been replaced by a large modern *cuvier* built in 1989. This is a medium-sized property and the fermentation tanks are relatively small. The grapes are pressed in a horizontal press, and the wine is aged for 18 months in 50 percent new oak in a functional *chai à barriques*.

The wine has a reputation for toughness, at least in its youth. That may have been the case in the past, but tastings of more recent vintages suggest that Lynch-Moussas is now styled as a rich fleshy Pauillac that can be drunk young. Although some wine fanciers look down their noses at Lynch-Moussas, it offers exceptional value.

CHÂTEAU LYNCH-MOUSSAS
Area under vine: 54 hectares
Grape varieties: 75% Cabernet Sauvignon, 13% Merlot, 12% Cabernet Franc
Average age of vines: 25 years
General director: Émile Castéja
Maître de chai: Olivier Guerin
Chef de culture: Bernard Coureau
Consultant oenologist: Pascal Ribéreau-Gayon
Oak ageing: 15 months in 50% new oak
Second wine: Château Haut Madrac
Average production: 18,000 cases

CHÂTEAU PÉDESCLAUX

This relatively small domaine was created in 1825 by Urbain Pédesclaux, a Bordeaux wine broker, who bought up plots of land close to what are now Grand-Puy-Lacoste and d'Armailhac. The present property consists of three parcels of vines: six hectares around the château north of the town of Pauillac between Le Pouyalet and the estuary; another six hectares south of Le Pouyalet; and a further parcel between Pauillac and Château Lynch-Bages.

In 1891 the estate was sold to the Comte de Gastebois, and in 1950 it came into the hands of the present owners, the Jugla family. Lucien Jugla had been renting the property from the Gastebois family since 1931 and was well entrenched. The Juglas have deep roots in the Médoc and trace their ancestry back to the fifteenth century. Bernard Jugla supposes that the family name is derived from *jongleur* and imagines that his medieval ancestors must have been troubadours. The grandfather of the present owner, Bernard Jugla, was for many decades the *régisseur* at Château Duhart-Milon. The family owns a number of other smaller properties in Pauillac, of which the best known is Château Colombier-Monpelou.

The lean and dapper Bernard Jugla has been running the family domaines since 1965, but he seems casual and relaxed about his occupation. Within their categories, both Pédesclaux and Colombier-Monpelou

are under-achievers. The wines are commercial and straightforward and have the merit of being relatively inexpensive.

The château is an unpretentious house on the eastern edge of Le Pouyalet. The ground floor is used for tastings and receptions and the upper storey is inhabited by Bernard's sister. The Pédesclaux vineyards are, on average, quite old, yet yields are high and Jugla sees no problem with harvesting a crop of 60 hectolitres per hectare, even after green-harvesting in June. The proportion of Petit Verdot in the vineyards is not always used in the wine. In the 1989 and 1996 vintages it did exceptionally well, but in weaker years such as 1992 and 1993 it was not included in the blend, presumably because of insufficient ripeness.

Until 1991 Pédesclaux was equipped with tanks of enamelled metal, but these have been replaced with stainless steel. Jugla favours a fairly warm fermentation, at up to 31 degrees Centigrade. In 1994 he began to encourage the malolactic fermentation in *barriques*, about half of which are new each year, where the wine remains for some 15 months.

Since 1983 the wine has been exclusively distributed through the large Bordeaux *négociant* CVGB. It is rarely encountered in Britain. Pédesclaux, along with Croizet-Bages, is the least impressive of the Pauillac *crus classés*. There is no reason why its well-located vineyards shouldn't produce excellent firm wines with good Pauillac typicity, and the fact that it does not do so seems to reflect the deliberate choice of the Jugla family to offer a more supple lightweight style.

CHÂTEAU PÉDESCLAUX
Area under vine: 20 hectares
Grape varieties: 65% Cabernet Sauvignon, 25% Merlot, 7% Cabernet Franc, 3% Petit Verdot
Average age of vines: 40 years
Technical director: Bernard Jugla
Maître de chai: Jean Jugla
Oak ageing: 15 months in 50% new oak
Second wine: Château Belle Rose
Average production: 8,000 cases

CHÂTEAU PONTET-CANET

This grand old property, neglected for much of its history, is now approaching the quality level expected from a domaine with vineyards neighbouring those of Mouton-Rothschild.

The property was established by Jean-François Pontet in 1725. Pontet was a politician who rose to high office as governor-general of the Médoc and secretary to King Louis XV. He was also the owner of Château Langoa-Barton, but it was sold to Hugh Barton in 1821 by his descendant, Bernard de Pontet. The estate remained in the hands of the Pontet family throughout the Revolution and beyond the classification of 1855. Given the large area of the vineyards and the high reputation of Pontet-Canet, it is surprising that it did not win a higher ranking.

In the 1860s the successors of Bernard de Pontet sold the estate to the distinguished Danish-German *négociant* Hermann Cruse. The Cruses remained proprietors through many generations, and constructed the large iron-beamed *cuvier*. Although they did much to improve the quality of the wine, it was sold exclusively through their Bordeaux business, and was either bottled in Bordeaux or shipped in cask to importers in various parts of the world. (This accounts for the large number of foreign bottlings encountered in tastings of older vintages. I recall a bottle of 1964 I bought many years ago with the words 'Shipped in wood by Cruse'

The interior of Château Pontet-Canet

Château Pontet-Canet

on the label.) The wine was also well known on the French railways, with whom the Cruses had negotiated a lucrative contract. For a time there was even a wine marketed as nonvintage Pontet-Canet, an aberration I have never encountered but reported by Clive Coates to be virtually undrinkable. No doubt its purpose was to mop up the production of poor vintages. Since 1972 all the wine has been château-bottled.

The 1974 wine scandal implicated the Cruse firm and forced the sale of the estate. The following year the property was bought by Guy Tesseron, a Cognac producer who was the proprietor of Château Lafon-Rochet in Saint Estèphe. Today both properties are run by his twin sons, Alfred and Michel. Ironically, Michel Tesseron is married to a member of the Cruse family, and relations between the Tesserons and the former owners seem very cordial.

The château is a fine nineteenth-century mansion set in a wooded park adjoining the offices and *chais* of the domaine. The ground floor is the service wing of the château, and the reception room and bedrooms are reached by an imposing central staircase. Today the château is used mostly for entertaining and as an occasional residence for Alfred Tesseron. It is one of the incidental pleasures of dining at Château Pontet-Canet that the Tesserons think it unremarkable to serve nineteenth-century Cognac after the meal.

This is a very large estate of almost 80 hectares, planted in two large parcels. The topsoil is gravel and the subsoil is composed of clay and limestone. The land is gently undulating and rises to a height of almost 30 metres. There are about 50 hectares around the château, and 28 hectares on the other side of the D2 road, sloping towards the estuary. This plot is planted mostly with Merlot, of which there is a good deal at Pontet-Canet. Although the average age of the vines is 27 years, young vines are consigned to the second wine, Les Hauts de Pontet, created in 1982. The average age of the vines used for the *grand vin* is 35 years, and at present between 45 and 60 percent of the château's production goes into that wine. The Tesserons issue detailed reports on each vintage, so it is easy to observe that average yields are around 55 hectolitres per hectare.

All harvesting is manual and up to eight sorters pick through the grapes at the winery, eliminating suspect bunches or berries. The *cuvier*, which dates from the beginning of the Cruse period of ownership, is one of the most imposing in Pauillac, with its rows of wooden vats that were used from 1865 to 1985. The Tesserons decided to stop using the vats because of difficulties they experienced lowering the temperature of fermentation if it rose too high. They like to pick as late as possible, and that means not taking any risks with the fermentation process. Now

The exterior of the cuvier at Pontet-Canet

fermentation takes place in stainless-steel tanks at temperatures between 25 and 30 degrees Centigrade.

However, the Tesserons are thinking of changing their minds once again. The *maître de chai* is keen to use the old cement tanks, used now only to stock wines, for fermentation. Although cement tanks have long been out of fashion in the Médoc, a growing number of winemakers are recognising their virtues, since they retain heat very well and permit a long, slow fermentation. At Pontet-Canet their use would be restricted to cooler vintages to avoid the risk of excessively high temperatures.

Although the quantity of press wine is small – usually about 4 percent and never more than 10 percent – the cellars are equipped with a pneumatic press. The Merlot undergoes its malolactic fermentation in *barriques*, the Cabernet varieties in stainless steel. The wine receives a lengthy ageing in *barriques*, of which half are new. After an eggwhite fining, the wine is given a light filtration and bottled.

The improvements in quality at Pontet-Canet can be attributed mainly to greater selection. As previously mentioned, all wine made from young vines ends up in Les Hauts de Pontet. This second wine is aged in older barrels for about 10 months, and the casks are stored in a humid underground cellar, built by the Cruses and a rarity in the Médoc. Michel Tesseron points out that the moist subterranean cellars are excellent for the wine, but wreck the barrels, so the *grand vin* is never aged here. There are plans, as yet unconfirmed, to age some of Les Hauts in new oak and create a third wine. The problem for Pontet-Canet, and for other estates, is that the second wine is of very good quality, especially in fine vintages, and sold too cheaply. Creating a third wine, as Latour and Lafite have done, opens the possibility of improving the quality of the second wine and charging a higher price for it.

Pontet-Canet is a rich Pauillac, powerful, complex, and with considerable depth of flavour. Despite the high proportion of Merlot in the blend (41 percent in 1994, 36 percent in 1995), Pontet-Canet doesn't have the sheer finesse of, say, Pichon-Lalande. Robert Parker, some years ago, described the wine as 'a sleeping giant', but opined that stricter selection and the picking of riper fruit would 'propel Pontet-Canet into the top echelon'. Consciously or not, the Tesserons have listened to that advice, and the wine is now of very high quality and ages extremely well.

CHÂTEAU PONTET-CANET
Area under vine: 78 hectares
Grape varieties: 62% Cabernet Sauvignon, 32% Merlot, 6% Cabernet Franc
Average age of vines: 27 years
Directors: Alfred and Michel Tesseron
Maître de chai: Alain Coculet
Chef de culture: Jean-Michel Comme
Consultant oenologist: Jacques Boissenot
Oak ageing: 15-22 months in 50% new oak
Second wine: Les Hauts de Pontet
Average production: 22,000 cases, plus 8,000 cases of Hauts de Pontet

OPPOSITE: *The oak vats of Pontet-Canet*

A gentle, gravelly slope in the Pauillac vineyards

The Other Wines of Pauillac

Because Pauillac is richly endowed with classified growths, some of them close to 100 hectares in size, there are not a great number of *crus bourgeois,* and those that do exist are often small. For commercial reasons, some have become obscure, being sold principally in specific markets such as the Netherlands or Belgium. Nonetheless, there are some very good *crus bourgeois* worth looking for, especially since prices tend to be reasonable.

If few of the *crus bourgeois* rise to the heights of the best classified growths, this is a reflection of two factors. First, the vineyards are not usually as well located, so the wines can be less consistent than those of châteaux with exceptionally well-exposed sites. Second, whereas the top growths, which fetch high prices for their wines, can afford to declassify up to 40 or 50 percent of their crop if maintaining quality demands it, this is not always possible for a *cru bourgeois* with a far smaller vineyard area. Nevertheless, the more quality-conscious *crus bourgeois* can and do maintain high standards by selling their least impressive wines to wholesalers. Moreover, small estates lack laboratories or cannot afford the very detailed analyses that have become routine at larger estates. This lack of technical acumen has led in the past to occasional secondary fermentation and other winemaking accidents.

There are also historical reasons for the small number of *crus bourgeois.* During the 1930s, when all the estates of the Médoc suffered both from the economic depression and from a series of disastrous vintages, many properties changed hands. For some owners it was a question of selling, even at a loss, or joining the cooperative.

The story of Château Haut-Bages Averous is typical. This estate belonged to the Averous family in the nineteenth century and was still an important property in the early years of the twentieth century, with about 20 hectares under vine. Mademoiselle Averous achieved local renown for her great piety. She apparently had a deal with the Bishop of Lourdes who, in exchange for a cask of her wine each year, dispatched a cask of holy water which the Mademoiselle would use to baptise newly planted vines. In the 1920s and 1930s the estate fell on hard times, like so many others in Pauillac. Various parcels were sold off to neighbours in an attempt to keep the property afloat. Finally, in 1973, the owner found himself with a mere three hectares, which happened to be adjacent to the Lynch-Bages vineyards. They were bought by the Cazes family who replanted the vineyards.

Haut-Bages Averous is now the second wine of Lynch-Bages, though of course the wine now includes batches from all parts of the vineyards, not only from the original three hectares. The rules permit estates to use a château name for the second wine if it refers to a specific property that has been absorbed by the larger estate. Thus although Haut-Bages Averous no

The autumn harvest near Tour d'Aspic

longer exists as an independent wine, the name lives on as what was left of the estate after it was purchased in its entirety by Lynch-Bages.

In the remainder of this chapter, second wines have been omitted as they have been discussed alongside the principal estate in the preceding chapters. Not all the wines presented here are *cru bourgeois*; some are without any classification, which is not necessarily a reflection on their quality. Château La Bécasse, for example, was refused the status of *cru bourgeois* merely because of its small size.

CHÂTEAU LA BÉCASSE ✌ The label of this excellent wine features the emblem of a woodcock, the game bird so avidly hunted by Georges Fonteneau, who founded this estate in 1966. His grandfather Louis had been the *régisseur* of Château Ducru-Beaucaillou in Saint Julien, and also owned a small property called the Cru de la Bécasse in the same commune. Georges Fonteneau exchanged this *cru* for some vineyards in Pauillac, which he named Château La Bécasse. The property is now run by Roland Fonteneau, the son of Georges. The cellars are tucked into a corner house in the hamlet of Bages.

A wine-stained barrel and glass bung

The vineyards are divided among 20 different parcels between the Bages plateau and the Pichon vineyards. The largest parcel is a single hectare opposite Château Cordeillan-Bages. There is a great deal of Merlot in the wine, and Roland Fonteneau is hoping to increase the proportion of Cabernet Sauvignon over the years, giving a more structured wine with greater Pauillac typicity.

The grapes are picked manually and given a three-week *cuvaison* with frequent pumping over. By the time the malolactic fermentation is complete, Fonteneau will have blended the wine. It is then aged in *barriques* for 18 months. Despite La Bécasse's modest appellation, Fonteneau uses between 25 and 40 percent new oak, depending on the ripeness of the vintage. Barrels no more than six years old are bought from estates such as Latour and Margaux, so that Fonteneau can be sure that they have been well maintained.

Fonteneau seems quite content with the present proportion of new oak in the *chai*, as he does not want a wine especially marked by new wood. The wines are fined with eggwhite and bottled without filtration.

In style La Bécasse is thoroughly traditional and is designed for patient cellaring. The wine has an excellent and well-deserved reputation and is modestly priced for the quality. Because of the limited production, the wine, although exported to many countries, is not always easy to track down, though it is usually available in the wine shops of Pauillac.

CHÂTEAU LA BÉCASSE
Area under vine: 4.2 hectares
Grape varieties: 55% Cabernet Sauvignon, 36% Merlot, 9% Cabernet Franc
Average age of vines: 35 years
Director and winemaker: Roland Fonteneau
Oak ageing: 18 months in 25-40% new oak
Average production: 2,500 cases

An old Merlot vine

CHÂTEAU BÉHÈRÉ ✌ This tiny domaine is a new enterprise as the owners, Jean-Gabriel and Anne-Marie Camou, only bottled their first vintage in 1994. The cellars occupy former stables along the road that leads from Le Pouyalet towards Mouton-Rothschild. The vineyards – some they own, others they rent – are divided between various plots: one near Clerc-Milon on the Pouyalet plateau; another on the Carruades plateau not far from Lafite; a third at Artigues not far from Château Pibran; and a fourth parcel, from which the estate takes its name, close to Château Bernadotte. In the 1920s this last parcel was known as Cru de Béhèré and belonged to the Comte de Ferrand, the former proprietor of Château d'Armailhac.

Jean-Gabriel Camou worked for many years as a *vigneron* at Lynch-Bages, but since 1977 has been patiently assembling his network of vineyards. Because the parcels are so disparate, the vines are of various ages, with some very old vines and others, in the majority, that were replanted by Camou. For many years he sold the estate's production to the cooperative, La Rose Pauillac, but in 1993 he began vinifying the wine with a view to selling it himself, although the 1994 is their first commercially available vintage.

Some of the production is still sold to wholesalers, but the Camous now keep the best for themselves. The Béhèré wines are fermented in steel tanks and aged in *barriques*. The proportion of new oak has increased from year to year, and in 1996 they used 45 percent. The wine is mostly sold locally.

Although the enterprise of the Camous has to be admired, it must be said that the wine is not very exciting, and even in a solid vintage such as 1994 it seems light and modest. Jean-Gabriel Camou is the first to admit that he is a *vigneron* rather than a winemaker, and is heavily dependent on the advice of his oenologist. In the future, no doubt, the Camous will gain in winemaking experience and confidence.

CHÂTEAU BÉHÈRÉ
Area under vine: 1.8 hectares
Grape varieties: 65% Cabernet Sauvignon,
32% Merlot, 3% Petit Verdot
Director and winemaker: Jean-Gabriel Camou
Oak ageing: 15 months in 40% new oak
Average production: 400 cases

CHÂTEAU BELLEGRAVE ✌ This handsome nineteenth-century château, partially obscured by walls and tall trees, is located along the main road in the village of Saint Lambert, opposite Château Fonbadet. The modern history of this *cru bourgeois* begins in 1901, when it was bought from Armand Roux by a Dutchman named Van de Voort. It remained in his descendants' possession until January 1997, when the family decided it was time to sell the property. On the death of the owner, he and his family were living in California, and no family member seemed prepared to take on the burdens of running the estate.

Château Bellegrave

The tasting room, Château Bellegrave

The new owner is Jean-Paul Meffre, whose family own a number of properties in the Médoc, notably Château Plantey in Pauillac. The vineyards consist of only three hectares, and the Meffres know little about the history of the property or how the wine was made under the Dutch régime. In the 1980s the vineyards were planted with 80 percent Cabernet Sauvignon, 15 percent Merlot, and 5 percent Petit Verdot.

It is too soon for the Meffres, who are still learning their way around the cellars beneath the château, to decide on questions of vinification and *élevage*. The wine fetches a high price so good quality should be expected.

CHÂTEAU BERNADOTTE ∾ Northern Europeans have always made a contribution to the Bordeaux wine trade, so it should come as no great surprise that, until quite recently, the owners of this estate were Swedes: hence the name of the château, borrowed from the Swedish royal family. The Eklunds arrived in the village of Saint Sauveur in 1973 and acquired a few vines, which were vinified at the local cooperative until they constructed a winery and *chai*. Bernardotte forms part of a larger estate, Château Fournas Bernadotte, where all the wine is now made.

In March 1997, the Eklunds sold the whole estate to May-Eliane de Lencquesaing of Château Pichon-Lalande. Madame de Lencquesaing explained that there is such strong demand for the second wine of Pichon-Lalande, the Réserve de la Comtesse, that she wants to add to her portfolio a more modest but well-made wine of the region. It is not clear why the Eklunds chose to sell when they did. Curt Eklund has a second career as an air-force pilot, and he and his wife were not always at the property and had to rely on the service of *régisseurs*.

Fournas Bernadotte is a *cru bourgeois* of the Haut-Médoc and consists of 26 hectares. The Pauillac portion of the estate, bought in 1983, comprises a further nine hectares in two main parcels: one mixed among the vineyards of Pontet Canet, Mouton-Rothschild, and Lafite; the other near Artigues. Although most of the vines were picked manually, the Eklunds also used a machine to harvest some of the crop.

Since 1988 the must has been vinified in stainless-steel tanks, where they enjoy a four-week *cuvaison*. The wine is aged in *barriques*, but the new-oak component is no more than 20 percent. The wine is fined and filtered before bottling.

Bernadotte is an attractive, well-balanced but unremarkable wine. It usually has good fruit and is not over-extracted. It is the view of the new owner that the production was never selective enough, so presumably future vintages should show greater concentration and depth of flavour.

CHÂTEAU BERNADOTTE
Area under vine: 9 hectares
Grape varieties: 63% Cabernet Sauvignon, 35% Merlot, 2% Cabernet Franc and Petit Verdot
Owner: May-Eliane de Lencquesaing
Oak ageing: 16 months in 20% new oak
Average production: 5,000 cases

CAVE COOPÉRATIVE: LA ROSE PAUILLAC ∾ It seems odd at first glance to find a cooperative among some of the most valuable vineyard sites in the world. Founded in 1933 with 52 founder-members during one of the worst periods in the economic history of the region, La Rose Pauillac was the first cooperative in the Médoc. Many growers and smaller estates found it impossible to survive independently, given the fall in worldwide demand and the run of poor vintages. Many growers were glad to throw in their lot with a cooperative that would undertake the vinification and marketing of their wines, freeing them to seek better-paying jobs away from the vineyards.

If the cooperative thrived during hard times, it has floundered during the last decade, when high prices persuaded some growers to vinify their own production rather than sell their grapes to the cooperative; others took advantage of soaring vineyard prices to sell rows and parcels to some of the larger estates. At present the cooperative is responsible for vinifying 78 hectares, considerably less than the surface owned by some of the classified growths. There are 118 participants, which means that some members own no more than a few rows of vines.

Cave Coopérative of Pauillac

The cooperative's cellars are at the northern end of the town of Pauillac. They have an old-fashioned appearance, and vinification still takes place in temperature-controlled cement tanks. The wines are then aged in older *barriques* for 18 months. Not all the wine is bottled, and some of the less impressive lots are sold off to *négociants*. The main label is La Rose Pauillac, but the cooperative also uses château labels: Haut Milon, Hauts de la Bécade, and Domaine des Gémeaux. The *cuvée* called Grand Coteaux de Papineau is sold to *négociants*.

Although the cooperative is of diminishing importance in Pauillac, it continues to make wines of acceptable quality. La Rose Pauillac does not have the concentration and flair of the best growths of the commune, but the wine does not lack typicity and best vintages can age well. The 1970 was still a good bottle of wine in 1997. The cooperative has a small tasting room and offers older vintages for sale at very modest prices.

CHÂTEAU COLOMBIER-MONPELOU ∾ This property is owned by Bernard Jugla, the proprietor of the fifth growth Château Pédesclaux. The winery can be seen among the vineyards on the right when driving from the commune of Saint Estèphe towards Pauillac. The Jugla domaines are very much a family business, with brother Jean involved as well as Bernard's son Denis, the export manager, and Bernard's son-in-law Patrick Ballion.

CHÂTEAU COLOMBIER-MONPELOU
Area under vine: 17 hectares
Grape varieties: 65% Cabernet Sauvignon,
25% Merlot, 5% Cabernet Franc,
5% Petit Verdot
Average age of vines: 25 years
Director and winemaker: Bernard Jugla
Oak ageing: 15 months in 40% new oak
Average production: 8,000 cases

The estate had a good reputation in the late eighteenth and early nineteenth century. It was highly rated in Armand d'Armailhacq's book on Bordeaux, but was not classified in 1855; however, in 1932 it was recognised as a *cru bourgeois supérieur*. The owners earlier in the twentieth century were the Desse family, who sold the estate in 1914 to a family of shippers and bankers named Adde. In 1945 the Addes sold the property to Roger Seurin, their *régisseur*; he ran into financial problems in the 1960s, and in 1970 Jugla bought the estate from him. By this time the château was detached from the estate. (Baron Philippe de Rothschild had bought the château in 1939 and transformed it into the headquarters of his *négociant* business, La Baronnie.)

Most of the vineyards are located near the winery, between the D2 and the vineyards of Châteaux Pontet-Canet and Pibran, with additional parcels near the hamlet of Artigues. The vines are planted on gentle gravelly slopes, many of which face south, so exposure is very good and the grapes tend to ripen early.

BELOW: *Château Colombier-Monpelou*

In the 1970s Jugla was an enthusiast for organic viticulture, but he seems to have lost the faith and felt constrained by all the rules and regulations imposed by associations of organic growers. He still insists that for the most part his farming remains organic.

The grapes are picked by machine as well as by hand. The must is vinified in stainless-steel tanks installed in 1986 and given a *cuvaison* of up to four weeks. Since 1995 Jugla has opted to complete the malolactic fermentation in *barriques*, of which some 40 percent are new. The wine is fined and filtered before bottling.

Unlike many *crus bourgeois*, Colombier-Monpelou is complemented by a second wine: Château Grand Canyon, which is both a selection of parcels (young vines and so forth) and less satisfactory lots. It too is aged in *barriques* but there is no new oak component. Other labels used by the Juglas are Châteaux Pey la Rose and de Coubersant. Jugla is also the owner of two other *crus bourgeois*, Châteaux Grand-Duroc-Milon and Belle-Rose. Pey La Rose encompasses six hectares, consisting of parcels assembled in the late 1970s, and is the property of Bernard's son, Denis. Grand-Duroc-Milon is a five-hectare estate planted with 60 percent Cabernet Sauvignon, 25 percent Merlot, and 15 percent Cabernet Franc. Belle-Rose is a six-hectare property near Pontet-Canet producing about 30,000 bottles of supple wines. These various labels represent *marques* favoured by particular clients in particular markets rather than wines with a strong individual identity.

Given the location of the vineyards and the fact that Bernard Jugla declassifies part of the crop every year, it is surprising that Colombier-Monpelou is not a better wine. Since his fifth growth Pédesclaux is unexciting, it is perhaps to be expected that his *cru bourgeois* will not set the sky ablaze either. However, Colombier-Monpelou has the merit of being very reasonably priced, and some older vintages are sold at the winery.

Barriques sealed with glass bungs

CHÂTEAU CORDEILLAN-BAGES ✌ This attractive estate is better known for its hotel and restaurant than for its wine, but the wine is by no means negligible. The seventeenth-century building was once the headquarters of Château Bellevue Cordeillan, a large estate classified as a *cru bourgeois* in 1932 with 20 hectares under vine at the beginning of the twentieth century. One of its owners had been Monsieur Hilaret, the manager of Château Lafite, who bought the estate in 1887, then sold it to the Billa family. By 1962 it had gone the way of so many other small domaines in Pauillac, with parcels sold off in a futile effort to remain

Château Cordeillan-Bages also serves as Pauillac's top hotel

afloat. One of the purchasers had been the Cazes family, and in 1985, in association with AXA Millésimes, they bought what was left of the estate. The château has been converted into the top restaurant of Pauillac, charging high prices for sophisticated cooking. The hotel attached to the château is now part of the prestigious Relais & Châteaux group.

The Cazes team vinifies the wine, which is aged in one-year-old *barriques*. Cordeillan-Bages has earned the wrath of Robert Parker, who discerns a tartness in the wine that I never have. It is, in fact, a typical Cazes-style wine, dark, deep, rich, and extracted, though without the finesse and vigour that are the expression of an exceptional *terroir*.

CHÂTEAU LA COURONNE ✍ This property is part of the Borie empire, owned by Madame de Brest-Borie, the sister of Jean-Eugène Borie of Château Ducru-Beaucaillou. It came into being in the 1870s and was assembled by the *négociant* Armand Lalande. The four hectares of vineyards are inland, just southeast of Château Batailley, and are planted with 70 percent Cabernet Sauvignon and 30 percent Merlot. Just under 2,000 cases are produced on average.

CHÂTEAU LA FLEUR MILON ✍ In the early twentieth century, this estate belonged to Auguste Tourteau, who sold it to André Gimenez. In the 1950s Gimenez expanded the property by buying up small parcels from elderly proprietors with no heirs. After his death his daughter inherited La Fleur Milon, which is now run by her husband Claude Mirande.

Mirande is immensely proud of the improvements he has made in the *chais*. A *bon vivant* and *raconteur* in his mid-sixties, he affectionately refers to his wife as 'ma petite dame', a form of address she tolerates with admirable equanimity. Their two sons are also involved in the estate: Yannick looks after the vinification on a daily basis, while Gilles supervises the vineyard management.

The winery, which welcomes visitors into its spacious tasting room, is located in the northern part of Le Pouyalet, and the vineyards lie to the east of the hamlet; many rows are adjacent to those belonging to Mouton. I have seen an old label from Auguste Tourteau's time in which the estate is placed between two châteaux named Lafite and Mouton, thus suggesting that his vines were ideally located between the two, but this is not quite the case. In general the soil is very stony, with a subsoil of gravel blended with sand or clay. Proximity to the estuary has had the benefit of lessening the risk of frost damage, and even in 1991 their vineyards were virtually unscathed, allowing them to make a wine

CHÂTEAU CORDEILLAN-BAGES
Area under vine: 2 hectares
Grape varieties: 80% Cabernet Sauvignon, 20% Merlot
Director and winemaker: Daniel Llose
Oak ageing: 12-15 months in 1-year-old oak
Average production: 1,000 cases

A Pauillac vineyard in spring

Château La Fleur Milon

CHÂTEAU LA FLEUR MILON
Area under vine: 13 hectares
Grape varieties: 65% Cabernet Sauvignon, 25% Merlot,
5% Cabernet Franc, 5% Petit Verdot
Average age of vines: 45 years
Director and winemaker: Claude Mirande
Maître de chai: Yannick Mirande
Chef de culture: Gilles Mirande
Oak ageing: 18 months in 30% new oak
Second wine: Château Buisson-Milon
Average production: 6,650 cases

without any chaptalisation in a difficult vintage. There are parcels of very old vines, some, according to Claude Mirande, up to 100 years old.

The grapes are harvested manually and fermented in lined cement tanks, favouring a submerged-cap technique during the three-week *cuvaison*. The Mirandes are understandably proud of their long *chai à barriques* with its arched aisles. Since 1995 La Fleur Milon has aged its wine in 30 percent new oak, but the majority of the barrels are two years old and purchased from Pichon-Lalande. Mirande favours a lengthy ageing process, then fines and filters the wine before bottling begins in the early summer. Although La Fleur Milon is well equipped, it lacks the capacity to bottle all its production at once, so there are two or three bottlings. Monsieur Mirande says that the wine is stored in tanks after its *élevage* in barrels is complete, resulting in little variation in style or quality between bottlings.

The estate is large enough for a second wine – Château Buisson-Milon. The label Chantecler-Milon is used for bottlings sold to Bordeaux *négociants*, but this is the same wine as La Fleur Milon.

Until recently, La Fleur Milon has been a sturdily old-fashioned Pauillac. Some deride its wines as rustic, and they do lack some elegance. Nonetheless they are authentic Pauillacs, with deep colours, smoky meaty aromas, and robust and spicy on the palate. They age extremely well, and older vintages reveal a real *gout de terroir*, reflecting the excellence of the vineyards and the density of flavour produced by old vines.

I find La Fleur Milon an underrated property. The wines may not have great flair, but their richness and meatiness are very impressive. Their typicity as old-fashioned Pauillacs cannot be doubted. I suspect the long experience and gusto of Claude Mirande and the more up-to-date know-how of his sons will produce more excellent bottles at reasonable prices.

CHÂTEAU LA FLEUR PEYRABON ❧ There is no use hunting around Pauillac for this estate, as its name refers to a parcel of vines owned by Château Peyrabon, a large old estate in Saint Sauveur, to the west of Pauillac. Peyrabon has a fine eighteenth-century château and was already well known for its wine before the 1855 classification.

Until the 1930s the owners were the Comtes de Courcelles. There followed a succession of different proprietors. In 1958 the property was sold to René Babeau, who died in 1976. Today it is his son Jacques who runs the property.

Château Peyrabon, owner of the vines which produce La Fleur Peyrabon

Jacques Babeau is a genial man, relaxed and courteous, very much at home in his lovely house and park. In 1958 only six hectares were in production, and René Babeau planted an additional 30 hectares. After he inherited the property, Jacques bought a further 20. The five hectares of Pauillac lie to the east of the château, on gravelly soil within the boundaries of the commune of Pauillac.

Although only half the vines are of Cabernet Sauvignon, there is a sizeable proportion of Cabernet Franc, so that Merlot does not dominate the wine. Part of the vineyard is picked by hand, part by machine. Babeau favours a long *cuvaison* of more than three weeks, but adopts the curious policy of both filtering and fining the wine before it goes into *barriques*. I have encountered this technique in the Douro region of Portugal, but only with wines that are immensely tannic and extracted and thus less likely to be emaciated by such treatments. I do wonder whether Peyrabon might not be a richer and more satisfying wine without this fining and filtration at such an early stage. The *élevage* is in 50 percent new oak. Babeau is an unashamed admirer of new oak, which is the only medium that gives the vanilla aromas and finesse that he likes in a wine. He prefers a medium toast to his barrels. The wine is sold mostly to private clients, so it is not easily encountered, but is worth seeking.

Vineyards near village of Le Pouyalet

CHÂTEAU FONBADET 🙜 Fonbadet has long been an insider's wine: well known and respected both within and beyond the Pauillac district as a reliable and consistent growth. Driving south through Saint Lambert, the château is on the right, a rambling nineteenth-century house set within an attractive walled park. The owner is Pierre Peyronie, a courteous white-haired man with a long experience of the region and its wines. His great-grandfather was the *régisseur* at Château Lafite, so his roots in Pauillac go deep.

The owner in the early nineteenth century was Pierre de Gères de Loupes, but by the end of the century the vineyards were broken up and dispersed. They remain this way, with some adjoining the château, others near Le Pouyalet and Mouton-Rothschild, still others within Pauillac itself.

Peyronie prides himself on the great age of his vines and the consequent low yields, which he believes is an essential component of a well-structured Pauillac. He claims that his yields never exceed 40 hectolitres per hectare, which is well below average. Monsieur Peyronie is conservative in the best sense, distrustful of viticultural 'progress' that does little for the quality of the wine, and he is wary of rootstocks that can be overproductive. He also refuses to replant entire vineyards, preferring to replace vines individually as they reach the end of their natural life.

The harvest is manual, and the *cuvaison* varies between two and four weeks, depending on the vintage. The old hydraulic press of the estate is still in use, and Peyronie is very satisfied with the quality of the press wine it gives. After ageing the wine for 18 months in his long dark *chais,* the wine is fined but bottled without filtration.

Peyronie and his delightful daughter Pascale run a rather complex commercial operation. Fonbadet is their flagship wine, but there are many other labels used for wines sold to *négociants*, including Châteaux Padarnac, Montgrand-Milon, Tour du Roc-Milon, and Haut-Pauillac. Sometimes the same wine or blend may appear under more than one label, depending, presumably, on exclusivity arrangements with the purchasers. Peyronie bought Haut-Pauillac in 1971, comprising five hectares of very old vines located close to Fonbadet. Château Padarnac also consists of five hectares close to Mouton-Rothschild.

CHÂTEAU GAUDIN 🙜 This old-fashioned property is located in Saint Lambert, on the left side of the road when driving south towards Bordeaux. The owner, Pierre Bibian, is now elderly, and the property is managed by his daughter, Madame Capdevielle. Her husband is a former stonemason who built some of the *chais* in the region including that at Château Pontet-Canet. It takes its name from a cooper, Guillaume

The entrance to Château Fonbadet

CHÂTEAU FONBADET
Area under vine: 16 hectares
Grape varieties: 60% Cabernet Sauvignon, 20% Merlot, 15% Cabernet *Franc, 5% Petit Verdot and Malbec*
Average age of vines: 55 years
Director and winemaker: Pierre Peyronie
Oak ageing: 18 months in 25% new oak
Average production: 6,000 cases

CHÂTEAU GAUDIN
Area under vine: 10 hectares
Grape varieties: 85% Cabernet Sauvignon,
10% Merlot, 5% Petit Verdot and Malbec
Average age of vines: 45 years
Winemakers: Capdevielle family
Oak ageing: 18 months in 2-year-old oak
(plus 10% new oak)
Average production: 500 cases

Gaudin, who bought the estate in 1858; his last descendant was killed in World War I. Pierre Bibian acquired the property in 1951 and for many years sold the production to the Pauillac cooperative. In 1968 he began to vinify and bottle the wine himself.

The vineyards are dispersed, though there is a single parcel of some three hectares; the remainder are located near Pichon-Longueville, near Lynch-Bages, and near Grand-Puy-Ducasse. Madame Capdevielle says that her vines are planted on excellent gravel soils, plus a little clay, and that there are parcels of vines that are up to 90 years old. The vineyards are dominated by Cabernet Sauvignon. Yields tend to be high, as the Capdevielles see no virtue in discarding what nature has been generous enough to produce.

No herbicides are used in the vineyards, and the grapes are picked by hand. At Gaudin they like a thorough extraction, and the *cuvaison* can last for four weeks, with fermentation temperatures rising to 32 degrees Centigrade. The wine is aged in older *barriques* (plus 10 percent new oak) and is not usually blended until the spring following the harvest. Only the wine they sell directly at the estate to private customers and restaurants is aged in oak; most of the production is aged in tanks and sold to *négociants*. It is the admirable policy of Madame Capdevielle to age the wines for three years before offering them for sale. Many older vintages are still available and prices are very reasonable.

BELOW: *A cottage near the village of Saint Lambert*

CHÂTEAU HAUT-BAGES-MONPELOU ❧ In the 1840s this estate was already the property of the Castéja family and consisted of some 14 hectares. Inheritance fragmented the property, and most of the vineyards became incorporated within part of Château Duhart-Milon. After World War II, Marcel Borie and his son-in-law Émile Castéja began the tricky task of reconstituting the property, which is now some 10 hectares, planted with 75 percent Cabernet Sauvignon and 25 percent Merlot. The average production is about 2,500 cases and is distributed by the *négociant* Borie-Manoux. The wine is said to be soft, forward, attractive, and inexpensive.

Rain clouds over the vineyards

CHÂTEAU HAUT-LINAGE ❧ To visit the tiny *chais* of Haut-Linage is to step back in time by a few decades. Jack Fardègue, a tall, grave, grey-haired man, is a retired insurance agent, so winemaking is a sideline. Nonetheless wine is in his blood: his grandfather was the *maître de chai* at Château Bellegrave, also in Saint Lambert, and his father a cooper at Château Latour. His tiny parcels of vines have always been in his family and are located close to those of Pichon-Longueville and Batailley. The grape varieties planted are 60 percent Cabernet Sauvignon and Cabernet Franc and 40 percent Merlot.

The cellars are located in a few cramped rooms in a stone house in the heart of Saint Lambert. The wine is fermented in an old wooden vat, after which Fardègue adopts the ancient method of sealing the top of the vat with plaster, and inserting a curved tube that leads into a pot of water. This allows any gas produced during the final maceration period to escape harmlessly without any oxidation of the wine. Fardègue buys two-year-old barrels from Château Lafite, and recalls a time when the wine would have been aged in barrel for three years, but he now conforms to modern practice and ages it for 18 months. He fines the finished wine with eggwhite and bottles it without filtration. At Haut-Linage there is no blending tank, so each barrel is bottled separately. The wine, of which some 1,500 bottles are produced, is sold mostly to private clients.

CHÂTEAU HAUT-LINAGE
Area under vine: 0.5 hectare
Grape varieties: 60% Cabernet Sauvignon and Cabernet Franc, 40% Merlot
Owner and winemaker: Jack Fardègue
Oak ageing: 18 months in 2-year-old oak
Average production: 250 cases

CHÂTEAU PIBRAN ❧ Since 1987 this well-reputed *cru bourgeois* has been owned by AXA Millésimes, and consequently is managed by Jean-Michel Cazes and Daniel Llose. This late nineteenth-century château and estate had formerly belonged to the Ardilley family and, since 1941, to the Billa family.

Since the vineyards were in poor shape, AXA largely replanted them and at the same time improved the drainage. They are well located,

Château Pibran

CHÂTEAU PIBRAN
Area under vine: 10 hectares
Grape varieties: 60% Cabernet Sauvignon, 30% Merlot,
10% Cabernet Franc
Director: Jean-Michel Cazes
Technical director: Daniel Llose
Oak ageing: 12 months in 1-year-old oak
Average production: 4,500 cases

adjoining those of Mouton-Rothschild, Pontet-Canet, and Lynch-Bages, with additional parcels near the village of Artigues and behind Château Grand-Puy-Lacoste.

The vinification is similar to that practiced at Lynch-Bages, but since the wine tends to be less structured, the *cuvaison* is shorter and no new oak is used. The wines are made at the capacious new facilities at Pichon-Longueville. Pibran provides the Cazes/Llose experience without requiring great expenditure. One finds a similar depth of colour and lushness, though not the structure and power of wines from Lynch-Bages and Pichon-Longueville.

CHÂTEAU PLANTEY ✍ Driving north in the direction of Pauillac and through Saint Julien, a vast and not very prepossessing shed-like *chai* comes into view. This is Château Glana, the property of the Meffre family, who are also the proprietors of Château Plantey. Gabriel Meffre was a nurseryman from the Vaucluse in Provence, and, oddly for a southerner, fell in love with the Médoc. In 1955 he bought Château La Commanderie in Saint Estèphe, then Château Plantey, followed by Châteaux Glana and Lalande in Saint Julien. Meffre died in 1993, and although his widow is now the owner of the properties, they are run by her sons Jean-Paul and Claude.

Plantey is quite a large estate, planted in a single large block to the west of Pontet-Canet on good gravel soil with drainage down towards the nearby woods and stream. There is a high proportion of Merlot in the vineyards. The Meffres use no herbicides on their vines.

This estate has always been run on commercial lines. The grapes are picked by machine, a practice Claude Meffre defends by pointing out that this allows them to work swiftly, so they are not tempted to pick before the grapes have attained full maturity. Nonetheless it is hard to see how the same selectivity and quality of fruit can be expected when picking by machine, even though in recent years machines have become far gentler in their handling of the vines.

The grapes are sorted at the *cuvier*, a modern structure close to the vineyard. Curiously, temperature control is somewhat primitive, although Meffre finds their heat exchangers work well enough. The *cuvaison* lasts some three weeks and the temperature is allowed to rise as high as 33 degrees Centigrade. About one-third of the crop, from the best parcels, is aged in barrels, the rest in tanks. In order to maintain low prices, the Meffres are reluctant to invest in costly *barriques*, but Claude Meffre seems well aware that Plantey will never be a high-ranking Pauillac without a more classic *élevage*. He hopes to construct a proper *chai à barriques* in the years ahead and purchase a more substantial number of new oak barrels. About two-thirds of the crop ends up as Plantey; the remainder is consigned to the second wine, Château Artigues.

The wine is sold exclusively by Grands Vins de Gironde, so Plantey has been tailored to the style this merchant seeks. Plantey certainly does not lack fruit, though the abundance of Merlot can lead in certain vintages to jamminess; but the soil is clearly of good quality and I detect no dilution in the wine, though it does lack finesse. Although Plantey is hardly a high flyer among the lesser growths of Pauillac, Claude Meffre appears to be well aware of its deficiencies and seems keen to correct them.

CHÂTEAU SAINT MAMBERT ❧ Approaching this tiny property, which lies between Château Haut-Bages-Libéral and the estuary, one sees a small chapel and, alongside it, a pen filled with contented Limousin cattle. Château Saint Mambert has established its winery and tasting room in the former chapel of the hamlet of Saint Mambert. In the eighteenth century Saint Mambert was part of the commune of Saint Julien, not Pauillac, but it is now part of the larger village of Saint Lambert.

The Reyes family are primarily cattle raisers, and until 1993 they sold the fruit from their vines to the cooperative. Since the vines are very well

CHÂTEAU PLANTEY
Area under vine: 26 hectares
Grape varieties: 50% Cabernet Sauvignon, 45% Merlot, 5% Cabernet Franc
Average age of vines: 27 years
Directors and winemakers: Jean-Paul and Claude Meffre
Maître de chai: Yannick Mirande
Ageing: One-third aged 12 months in older *barriques*, the rest in tank
Second wine: Château Artigues
Average production: 15,000 cases

The grounds of Château Saint Mambert

Château Saint Mambert

located, they decided to vinify and market their own wine. Because of the small quantities, all the grapes are vinified together in stainless-steel tanks. (This is not often a satisfactory method, as the varieties do not usually ripen at the same time. With Cabernet Sauvignon the dominant variety, it can happen that the Merlot, left on the vine while the Cabernet ripens, can be overripe by the time it is picked.)

The grapes are sorted both in the vineyard and at the *cuvier* to eliminate fruit that is not up to standard. After fermentation the wine goes immediately into *barriques* where malolactic fermentation takes place. At present the Reyes use about 30 percent new oak, the remainder of the barrels being one-year old, but they hope to raise the percentage of new oak to 50 percent.

The Reyes are image-conscious, and the presentation of Saint Mambert has none of the dowdiness of properties such as Gaudin or Haut-Linage. They use expensive corks and pack their wines in wooden cases. Nonetheless, the prices are very reasonable. Despite the difficulties explained earlier relating to the harvesting, and the constraint against making a severe selection when the crop is so small, the wines are good.

CHÂTEAU SAINT MAMBERT
Area under vine: 0.75 hectare
Grape varieties: 65% Cabernet Sauvignon, 25% Cabernet Franc, 10% Merlot
Average age of vines: 40 years
Director and winemaker: M. Reyes
Oak ageing: 18 months in 30% new oak
Average production: 300 cases

CHÂTEAU LA TOURETTE ❧ Driving out of Pauillac on the D206, heading southwest past Château Batailley, the departure from the commune of Pauillac is marked by passing the hefty nineteenth-century château of Larose-Trintaudon, one of the largest domaines in the Médoc, specialising in soundly made commercial wines. The domaine is particularly proud of its rows of vines just over the border in Pauillac, although as I stood there with winemaker Franck Bijon it was hard to discern much difference in soil or exposure between two parcels of vines – one Pauillac, the other Haut-Médoc – separated by a track across the gravel.

The parcel in Pauillac is known as La Tourette and is vinified separately as the top wine of Larose-Trintaudon. The vines are planted on a gravel *croupe*, four metres deep, with a subsoil of gravel and clay. Some vineyards of Pichon-Longueville and Lynch-Bages lie close by. Bijon and his team lavish a care on La Tourette that they cannot afford to give to their Haut-Médoc. Foliage is removed in summer to assist healthy ripening, picking is delayed till the grapes are fully ripe, and the harvest is manual. Yields rarely exceed 53 hectolitres per hectare.

La Tourette is vinified in small stainless-steel tanks. Bijon likes a very long *cuvaison* of some five weeks, but to balance that he has to adopt modest temperatures and not pump over too often. The malolactic fermentation takes place in new oak barrels where the wine remains for 15 months. The toast of the barrels varies according to the vintage; thus in 1993 the toast was lighter than in 1995 or 1996. After bottling the wine is kept in the cellars for a further 18 months before being released.

CHÂTEAU LA TOUR PIBRAN ❧ At one time this *cru bourgeois* formed part of Châteaux Pibran, but became detached. The present owner is Jean-Jacques Gounel, a genial, middle-aged, bearded man. Originally one of the Castéja-owned properties in Pauillac, La Tour Pibran was by the early twentieth century under the ownership of a Belgian family named Ardilley.

After World War I, and especially during the 1930s, the fortunes of the estate declined and the Ardilleys sold La Tour Pibran following World War II. The new owners were the Gounels, formerly cattle raisers in the Médoc, but with no prior experience in wine production. When the Gounels bought La Tour Pibran, there were no vines left and they have gradually replanted the vineyards. In 1970 there were only six hectares in production; today there are 9.5 hectares and this might rise to 11 in a few years. Two-thirds of the vines are close to the uninhabited

CHÂTEAU LA TOURETTE
Area under vine: 3 hectares
Grape varieties: 80% Cabernet Sauvignon, 20% Merlot
Average age of vines: 30 years
Winemaker: Franck Bijon
Oak ageing: 15 months in 100% new oak
Average production: 1,600 cases

Detail, Château La Tour Pibran

Beret, cigarette, grapes . . .

château, and one-third is about one kilometre away. In all there are six parcels, some close to Châteaux d'Armailhac and Pontet-Canet.

Harvesting at La Tour Pibran is manual, and yields are close to the maximum. *Triage* takes place in the vineyard and the must is fermented in small temperature-controlled tanks. Gounel favours a fairly short fermentation and heats the must to get it started. The *cuvaison* is usually between 15 and 18 days. The wine is aged in two-year-old *barriques*. Gounel has no new oak because he sees no point in having just a few new barrels; he prefers the consistency his older barrels impart. There is a fining and light filtration before bottling. From the 1970s onwards the entire production has been sold in bottle.

There is no second wine at La Tour Pibran, and the wine is distributed by the Compagnie Médocaine des Grands Crus. La Tour Pibran is a one-man band – Monsieur Gounel – and is not set up to receive visitors. Gounel's aim is to make well-rounded wines that can be enjoyed young.

CHÂTEAU LA TOUR PIBRAN
Area under vine: 9.5 hectares
Grape varieties: 60% Cabernet Sauvignon, 32% Merlot, 8% Cabernet Franc and Petit Verdot
Average age of vines: 20 years
Director and winemaker: Jean-Jacques Gounel
Oak ageing: 15 months in 2-year-old oak
Average production: 6,000 cases

Cabernet Sauvignon before washing and destemming

Autumn sunlight in a Pauillac vineyard

Tasting Notes

◈

The following tasting notes are not intended to be a definitive and seamless assessment of the wines mentioned. Wine is a living, constantly changing product, and a tasting note is the outcome of a particular moment in time subject to all manner of subjective influences.

These impressions will, I hope, contribute in more subtle form to my assessments of the various estates and provide sketches of the wines they produce. Of all the wines of Bordeaux, those from Pauillac are the slowest to evolve and tasting notes about them tend to be more consistent than they often are when attached to the wines of other regions.

LAFITE-ROTHSCHILD

The great nineteenth-century vintages of Lafite included the 1810, 1848, 1864, 1869, 1874, 1875, 1895, and 1899, followed in this century by the 1900, 1906, 1920, 1924, 1929, (the 1928 was marred by secondary fermentation after bottling), and the 1934. The 1945, 1947, and 1949 (still exquisite when I drank it in 1997 at the château) were all great, as was the 1953. The 1955 (firm, stylish, and long in 1987) was outclassed by the sumptuous, hard-to-fault 1959 and 1961.

I have had differing experiences with the 1962: fully mature and drying on the palate in 1990, but more stylish and well balanced when drunk in 1993. (Bottling variations, no doubt.) In 1964 Lafite picked too late to save the crop from rain. The 1970 has no great reputation, but I was hugely impressed when I tasted it twice in the 1980s. It was a classic wine, not weighty but delicious in flavour and very stylish. The 1978, in my experience, is better than its reputation, with a complex and classic nose.

The 1982 is outstanding, immensely concentrated and full-bodied for Lafite, but the 1983 remains austere and lacking in the Lafite charm. The same is true of the 1985, but it has real Pauillac typicity and a great deal of tannin that needs time to soften. The 1986, marked by new oak and intensity, is a greater wine, but requires patience. The trio of 1988, 1989, and 1990 are superb at Lafite, but they remain discreet wines, lean rather than sumptuous, supple and elegant. Of the three, it is likely that the gorgeous 1989 will mature much faster than the other two. The 1994 is very good but 1995 could be destined for greatness.

The Carruades can be an excellent wine, especially in an outstanding vintage, but sometimes the Lafite leanness, when translated into the style of the lesser Carruades, can lack the support of fruit that the *grand vin* usually offers. However, in vintages such as 1988, 1989, and 1995 the second wines from Lafite can be brilliant. But in harder vintages such as 1993, when even the *grand vin* can be a bit tough and charmless, Carruades does not shine.

LATOUR

Like the other first growths, Latour has had poor years. At Latour this occured in the late 1970s and early 1980s, but by the late 1980s, the estate was back on top form.

The oldest Latour I have tasted is the 1940, which exhibited a meaty, cedary nose, and massive fruit before declining in the glass. Earlier vintages of outstanding quality include the 1811, 1815, 1844, 1858, 1864, 1865, 1870, 1878, 1893, 1899, 1900, 1904, 1920, 1926, 1928, 1929, and 1934. The 1945 and 1947 have a tremendous reputation, and I was overwhelmed by the 1948, which remained dense and powerful and full of life – an exemplary Latour. The 1949 is one of the loveliest clarets I have ever encountered, an exquisite wine, very concentrated and long. It is lighter in colour with cigar-box aromas and perfect balance and elegance on the palate. The 1952, tasted in 1986, looked and smelt healthy but was tiring and dry on the palate. The 1955 is more alive, with a vigorous nose and mouth-filling concentrated fruit. The 1957 and 1958 are examples of Latour's success in off years.

A harvester at work

The 1959 Latour is a classic claret, showing depth, power, concentration. (I have encountered bottle variation in the 1959, with one bottled sampled being excessively evolved.) The 1961 has a sensational reputation, but, alas, has never passed my lips. If it's better than the big, spicy 1962, then it must be a tremendous wine. Like many top 1961s, it has not yet reached its peak. The 1964 is very good but still tough, a tannic and burly wine that remains rather closed 30 years after the vintage; in that rainy year Château Latour benefitted from its ability to pick early. The 1965 is an easygoing wine, quite a success for a rot-tainted vintage. The 1966 is outstanding and still full of life, and the 1967 is remarkably good for the vintage and is now drinking well.

The 1970 is a real blockbuster, a massive Latour, powerfully structured and with a rich core of fruit and tannin. It remains youthful and will undoubtedly become a great and sumptuous wine. The 1971 does not have a great reputation, but on the one occasion I tasted it I found it sumptuous, although far more evolved than the 1970. The 1973 is an agreeable wine, with a seductive cedary nose

and surprising structure for the vintage; it will not improve further. The 1975 has an excellent reputation, but its powerful tannins need time to soften. The 1976 is disappointing, with the baked character of the year. The 1978, and to a lesser extent the 1979, are both very good and still youthful. The 1980 is charmless, and the 1981, if not an outstanding wine, is a success for the vintage.

The 1982 has all the power, opulence, and class one would hope for in such a vintage. The tannins, unusual for a relatively young Latour, are fairly soft, and the wine is surprisingly approachable. The 1983 is a disappointment, lacking weight; it has style, even a certain raciness, but is scarcely a triumph for Latour. The 1985 is very fine, but, again, one expects more from a Latour; it is spicy, concentrated and chewy, but lacks the weight and complexity of Latour at its best. (Other tasters have been far more enthusiastic about the 1985.) I have not tasted the 1986 but it is widely considered a disappointment, lacking the power and structure that is a hallmark of this vintage. The 1988 seems lean and firm, but this is a backward year and the best wines are still closed; nonetheless, on the one occasion I tasted the wine, in 1995, it didn't seem to have the potential to be a great Latour.

Of the two great succeeding vintages, the 1990 outshines the 1989 and is likely to develop into one of the outstanding Latours. Significantly, it marks a return to the classic Latour style after the apparent lightening up of the 1980s. The 1991 is a great success for the vintage, no doubt largely thanks to the estate's escape from frost damage in the spring. Both 1992 and 1993 have good reputations, given these unmemorable vintages. The 1994 is superb – dense and silky, with great finesse and length. The 1995, tasted from cask, is truly sumptuous, with huge extract and impeccable balance. The 1996 may prove even better.

As for Les Forts de Latour, I have enjoyed outstanding bottles in the top vintages. As with most second wines, it offers fewer rewards in off years when even the *grand vin* is unable to deliver anything stunning in the glass. Nonetheless, Les Forts at its best is a splendid wine, a true cousin of Latour. It is worth reflecting that Latour, perhaps more than most other great wines of the Médoc, has an ability to develop harmony and complexity when those qualities are not apparent in the wines when young. Although my own experiences of vintages such as the 1986 and the 1988 have not been particularly positive (bearing in mind that we are talking about a first growth), I am quite prepared to believe that, as other tasters suggest, these vintages are developing into superb wines. If ever there were a wine to take a chance on, ignoring vintage reputations and occasional unflattering tasting notes, it has to be Latour. If it does not impress when young, just keep it another decade and see how it develops in bottle.

MOUTON-ROTHSCHILD

I have not had the privilege of tasting very old bottles of Mouton-Rothschild, but the 1878, 1900, 1928, 1929, 1934, 1937, 1945, 1947, 1949, and 1953 all have outstanding reputations. I have twice drunk the 1955, and one bottle was slightly superior to the other. Both had that typically rich, full-to-the-rim ruby-red colour of Mouton, and a nose of ultra-ripe Cabernet fruit tinged with exotic spices such as cloves. On the palate, it was utterly delicious, spicy and complex with incomparable breed. The 1959, tasted in 1987 and 1988, was equally profound in colour, with typical Mouton cedariness on the nose and palate; it's a forceful wine, charging through all the nooks and crannies of the palate, ending with a long vigorous finish. It wasn't showing any signs of age, nor of the alcoholic burn that afflicts some other 1959s. The 1961 is surely one of the great wines of that remarkable vintage, with a voluptuous yet elegant and classic nose, and wonderful depth of flavour – a dashing wine enjoyable at 30 years of age but still holding plenty of flavour and complexity in reserve. The 1962 is not far behind, another ultra-refined cedary wine, which struck me as graceful and perfectly tuned when I drank it in 1987.

Sunlight on trellis wires

The 1964, however, is relatively unsuccessful, pleasant and far from dry on the palate, but thin for Mouton and lacking in length. Far better is the 1966, though a bottle drunk at the château in 1993 was far more austere and tannic than one I recall from the late 1980s, which was lush and succulent. The 1970 is a very good wine, but not a great Mouton. I have always given it a good note, but it doesn't have quite the power and concentration of Mouton at its best. I have conflicting notes on the 1971 – perhaps bottle variation – but my jottings suggest that it is a wine to drink fairly soon. The 1975, tasted once, is hardly a hedonistic Mouton. It may yet improve, but the tannic dryness on the palate is striking and worrying. The 1976, a much maligned vintage, is very good: sweet and plump, with little of the baked character that mars many wines of this vintage, though it does lack elegance.

The 1978 is slightly disappointing, though that is true of so many wines from a vintage so enthusiastically welcomed when it first became available. The 1978 has a splendid attack, a mellow nose, and good acidity, yet doesn't develop much complexity in the mouth. The 1979 is stylish but rather light and pallid; the 1980, more predictably, also lacks concentration. Strangely, the 1981 is disappointing too: quite elegant on the nose, but lacking structure and breed on the palate, a merely acceptable wine from a modest year. The 1982 was wonderful in its youth: a great concoction of ripe fruit, oak, a kind of sumptuous earthiness, and remarkable concentration. When last tasted, in 1990, it was beginning to close up. Its greatness was still evident – such superb depth of flavour and brilliant length – but it is time to leave the 1982 alone for some years until its full dazzling potential is realised.

The 1983 also showed very well in its youth. It is a lovely 1983, classic and focused and finely balanced, and with a vibrant oaky nose. By 1990 it, too, was closing up and showing less well than when it had its baby fat; no doubt it will come round in another decade or so. The 1985 is easily eclipsed by the great 1986, another wine of immense girth and richness. It will be fascinating to taste

The park at Mouton-Rothschild

this alongside the 1982 in years to come. The 1987 is a success for the vintage, which is not saying a great deal, but it is polished, oaky, and stylish, though it doesn't have much length or richness.

The 1988 is a very backward wine, like so many in that austere vintage, but its concentration and richness and chewy texture suggest that it will be excellent – in time. The 1989, which I have not tasted, is thought by many to be over-oaked, but that character may well diminish with more bottle age. The 1990 is a lovely wine, smoky and elegant on the nose, with a silky texture and considerable finesse, but it is by no means one of the top wines of this remarkable vintage. Though still very young, it just doesn't seem to have the complexity and depth of flavour one would hope for, but it may evolve happily.

The vintages of the early 1990s were surprisingly classic given the difficulties of the harvest; even the 1992 is a well-structured, chunky wine with a future. The 1993 and 1994, which I have not tasted, were not well received. With 1995 Mouton showed itself to be back on top form, and the 1996 is also very promising, but final judgment must be reserved until the wines have been bottled.

PICHON-LALANDE

Great old vintages of Pichon-Lalande include 1875, 1893, 1900, 1918, 1921, 1924, 1928, and 1929. After the death of her husband, in 1990, Madame de Lencquesaing auctioned some older vintages of the wine in London, where I was able to taste such rarities as the 1925 and 1931. She was probably right to unload those particular vintages as they were fading fast, though vestigial fruit remained. The 1937 has a good reputation though did not show well, but the 1940 was a delight: very cedary on the nose with abundant charm on the palate and very good length. The 1942 was even more aromatic but showed astringency on the palate. The 1945 was an exceptional vintage at Pichon-Lalande, as elsewhere in Pauillac. The excellent 1947 and 1949 are by now mature. The 1952 and 1953 are said to be very fine, but I have not tasted them.

The 1955, however, remains delicious, a plump but vigorous wine with good length; it is ready to drink. The 1957 is typical of the vintage – in other words, a bit tough and lean, but enjoyable if drunk with food that softens tannins. The 1959 and 1961 are outstanding, and so is the very stylish 1962. The 1966, tasted twice in recent years, is a great success, with a seductive cedary nose, ripe and elegant, and delicious fruit on the palate, minty and with a fine acidity that is not astringent. The 1967 shows the deficiencies of the vintage; it's pleasant enough but should not be kept longer.

The 1970 is a quintessential Pichon-Lalande: a wonderfully perfumed nose, rich and spicy on the palate, no blockbuster but an elegant wine with good length. It is far less evolved than the 1971, which in 1990 had developed notes of tea and Bovril, not the most entrancing flavours in a fine wine. The 1975 is a great success for the vintage, tougher and more powerful than is customary with Pichon-Lalande, but by no means dry or over-tannic. The 1976 is now mature: a rounded supple wine with little of the baked character of this very hot vintage; it even has elegance, a rarity in 1976. Considering that 1977 was a year when the fruit failed to ripen properly, Pichon-Lalande's bottling was surprisingly harmonious and drinkable. I last tasted this wine 10 years ago and doubt that it has improved.

The 1978 was an excellent year for Pichon-Lalande, delivering a wine with a little more weight and structure than usual, yet balanced and complex; it should keep well. The 1979 is more discreet and charming, with sweet cassis fruit on the nose. The 1980 was good for the year, which isn't saying much, but the 1981 is one of the best wines of that attractive vintage, showing great finesse on the nose and a delicate spiciness on the palate. It is ready to drink but could be kept. The 1982 had an almost Californian voluptuousness when young, but in the 1990s has shown more classic features. It's an impeccable wine, marrying opulence and splendour with superb concentration and depth of flavour. The 1983 is also extremely good, with aromas of cedar and bacon; on the palate it remains concentrated and vigorous, with a marked acidity. The 1985 is marked by new oak on the nose, supple and rich on the palate, with nicely integrated tannins – a wine with no rough edges. The 1986, as one would expect, is tannic and powerful, and unlike many wines from this property, not really drinkable young. It will take time for its denseness and power to translate into the rich cedary style of a mature Pichon-Lalande.

The 1988 is evolving beautifully. When I blind-tasted a whole range of 1978s from the Médoc, this was one of the stars: very pure on the nose, a touch cedary, and stylish and assertive on the palate. It's not especially weighty, but has all the finesse one could wish for in a classic claret. I have not yet tasted the 1989, but was slightly disappointed with the 1990, which seemed surprisingly forward and lacking in power and structure for such a magnificent vintage. It has a silky texture, sumptuous fruit, but where's the complexity? The succeeding vintages of the 1990s also lacked some weight and density, but one has to remember that this is the Pichon-Lalande style, and is not a wine with the same kind of structure as Latour or Pichon-Longueville. Nonetheless, the 1995 seems exceptional and should develop gracefully in the bottle.

PICHON-LONGUEVILLE

The oldest Pichon-Longueville that has come my way is the 1955. Of the major postwar vintages before 1955, it is the 1949 and 1953 that seem to be holding up best. The 1955 was fairly lean and lacking in fruit, not a wine for keeping. The 1957 was a pleasant surprise – a sweet spicy wine, firmly structured but with delicious fruit, marred only by a dry finish. However, the same wine tasted two years later, in 1994, was less impressive, with high acidity. I suspect there may have been considerable bottle variation with this property at this time.

My notes on the 1961 are more positive than those I have encountered from other tasters. My example was bottled in England and may well have been superior to the château-bottled wine. It was certainly a delicious wine 30 years after the vintage – very stylish on the nose, and intense and positive on the palate, with remarkable length. Thereafter I have tasted no Pichon-Longueville until 1978. However, the very comprehensive notes by the British wine expert Clive Coates on just about all the intervening vintages suggest I have not missed a great deal.

The 1978 was delicious about 10 years after the vintage, and already mature, with overripe aromas and a plump fruitiness on the palate. More recently it has become looser and more astringent, and should be drunk. There's a touch of astringency on the 1979 by now, but it has a fine opulent Cabernet nose, and is surprisingly lively and vigorous on the palate. The 1982 is bursting with fruit, but unfortunately it is fruit of a rather jammy kind. Although not a bad wine, it pales in comparison with most other 1982s from top estates in Pauillac.

That same jamminess recurs in the 1985, which is a soft, precocious wine, not complex but lush and even sumptuous. Despite the machine-harvesting, the overall quality since the late 1970s suggests that the Bouteilliers were at last making some efforts to improve the quality of their underperforming wine. The 1986, which I have not tasted, is said to be very good. The 1987 was green and not attractive.

With the 1988, Pichon-Longueville takes a qualitative leap. It's a wine I have tasted on many occasions and it seems to gain in stature as it matures. When last tasted in 1997 it had an oaky chocolate and cassis nose of real depth. On the palate it was sumptuous, spicy, and powerful, yet with a purity and persistence of fruit flavours. The 1989 is great, too, and despite its evident oakiness has breed and style. On the palate, it has an overwhelming richness and lushness and concentration; it will take years before those abundant flavours of blackberry and cassis and oak amalgamate. The 1990 is in the same mould, a wonderfully fleshy wine, but it has greater elegance – a seductive wine of dazzling length.

The 1991 is a triumph for the vintage, easily one of the top wines of this awkward year. Dense and chunky, it lacks some finesse, but there is no denying the richness of fruit. The 1992 is

The alchemy of wine and oak

lighter, a more supple wine of reasonable concentration, but is not destined for a very long life. The 1993 is very marked by Cabernet and new oak. Although quite stylish on the nose, it is austere on the palate and lacks depth. Opulence is the hallmark of the 1994, a full-bodied fleshy wine confirming that some exceptional wines were made in this somewhat maligned year. Yet it seems outclassed by the brilliant 1995, at least on the basis of a cask sample.

DUHART-MILON-ROTHSCHILD

The oldest Duhart-Milon I have encountered was the 1976. Earlier vintages seem thin, though Clive Coates records enthusiastic tasting notes of the 1926 and 1929. The 1976 is not bad for the vintage, but is probably in decline. Duhart-Milon seems to have performed well enough in the classic vintages of 1978, 1982, and 1985, although the wines apparently lack excitement. The 1986 remains youthful, but has excellent potential. There are damsons and chocolate on the nose, typical of Cabernet Sauvignon, while the palate remains dense

and tarry. It is very Pauillac, and nicely concentrated, and will need quite a few years before it is fully mature.

The 1988 is impressive but not especially seductive. It has the same chocolatey tones as the 1986 but is more austere and unyielding, lacking finesse. It still has plenty to offer, but is unlikely ever to be a wine that will set the pulses racing. The 1989 is burly and powerful, another wine for the long haul, but with less breed than the excellent 1990. The 1990 remains very Duhart in its chunky structure, but also displays new attributes: a more fleshy texture, a more marked new-oak component, all contributing charm as well as power. The 1993 was, like so many wines of that difficult vintage, almost entirely composed of Cabernet Sauvignon, and was well received. The 1995, tasted from cask, was impressive, with a strong resemblance to the 1990, although, not surprisingly, with more assertive tannins at this stage.

In its youth, the concentrated 1996 is impressive, too, and may prove to be one of the bargains of a pricey vintage. Duhart seems to be gaining in stature each year.

D'ARMAILHAC

The oldest vintage I have drunk was the 1941. Harvest conditions were cold and the vintage has no great reputation. The wine was past its best: a caramelised nose of stewed apples, and on the palate dry and losing both fruit and length, but it remained very drinkable. The 1961 and 1978 are said to be excellent, but I could work up little enthusiasm for the 1979, which was very dry on the palate and lacked both power and interest. The 1981 was surprisingly hard and firm, an atypical Mouton-Baronne-Philippe, but showed a good deal of concentration and length. I have not encountered the well-regarded 1982 but the 1983 is already showing some age, with Bovril and liquorice on the nose, a frail palate lacking weight and richness. It is redeemed by an attractive acidity on the finish.

The 1985 is said to have the charm and fleshiness of that delightful vintage, and the 1986 is relatively light for a full-throttled year. The 1988 is evolving into an attractive bottle, with charming blackberry fruit on the nose and a vigorous attack, though lacking in concentration. As yet, I have not been impressed by the 1989, which although lush and tannic, seems to lack a core of fruit and is a little clumsy. The 1990 is very good, though not great: a rich silky wine with some of the Mouton opulence, though not the Mouton complexity. There is an overripeness in the 1990 that robs it of some elegance. The 1991, tasted soon after bottling, struck me as a success for the vintage, showing some youthful austerity but well balanced. The 1993 is attractive but simple, a pretty wine for short-term drinking. In cask the 1996 seems plump and sumptuous, remarkably fleshy for such an adolescent wine.

BATAILLEY

Old vintages of Batailley with a good reputation include 1928, 1934, 1945, and 1953. Despite the lacklustre reputation of Batailley, the 1959 was still going strong when I tasted it in 1993. The colour was surprisingly fresh, although the nose was more evolved, with some farmyard nuances, and the palate was not exactly elegant. Instead it had the roasted flavours of the vintage, ample alcohol, and ample vigour on the finish. The 1961 is still delicious and stylish, with marked coffee aromas and flavours. The 1964 was disappointing, and beginning to crack up by 1982. The 1970 is said to be pleasant and lively, if without much depth or richness. I have found the lesser 1971 vintage enjoyable; ripe and piquant on the nose, and on the palate soft and spicy but still lively. The 1979 had the softness typical of mature Batailley, and plenty of positive curranty fruit; it has developed fast and should be drunk soon. The 1981, in contrast, is a delicious wine, with sweet seductive Cabernet fruit and spicy tannins on the palate; it had impeccable balance and is a great success for the vintage.

The 1982 is relatively less successful. It has plenty of richness and ripeness on the nose but lacks complexity and power. Soft and plump, it would he hard to pick it out as a Pauillac from this remarkable vintage. The 1983 is also pleasant but undistinguished, lacking flair and bite. I recently tasted the 1988 blind and my note seems to reflect the Batailley style (or lack of it): 'juicy, quite generous but loosely structured, lacks grip, succulent, tangy but not elegant – still, it's enjoyable.' The 1989 is more impressive, with a lovely nose, a velvety texture, and great harmoniousness. But it lacks vigour and flair; the softness is peculiar on such a young wine from a mighty vintage. The 1990 seems in a similar mould. The 1992 is a fairly light, delicate, and elegant wine, but needs to be drunk young. At this stage it seems superior to the slightly green 1993.

CLERC-MILON

To date, the oldest Clerc-Milon I have encountered was the 1973, when the influence of the Rothschild régime could hardly have been discernible. At 20 years old it was remarkably robust, especially since the year was a light one. I have not tasted the wines made during the rest of the 1970s. However, the 1981 is quite light, lacking flesh and character. The 1982, hard and tough in its youth, has mellowed into a rich plump wine, with the ultra-ripe character of the vintage. It lacks finesse, but shows Pauillac character and has plenty of life left in it.

The 1983 is ready to drink, an elegant cedary wine, slightly lacking in concentration. The 1986 is gorgeous, with massive cassis fruit on the nose, and fine texture and balance and length. Ready now, it will keep well. The 1988 is a great Clerc-Milon, still rather closed, but with considerable complexity and depth of flavour. It should have an excellent future. The 1990 is sumptuous

The slow evolution in bottle

A cluster of Merlot

pointing: quite elegant on the nose, but forward and light. The 1993 was a feeble effort, even allowing for the difficulties of the vintage. The 1994 is not much better: a simple wine, tannic yet unstructured, and lacking length. The 1995 is a great improvement, and is the first wine to show the consequences of Jean-Louis Camp's corrections. The nose is ripe and charming, and the palate has some richness – not a great wine, but attractive and well balanced. The 1996 has similar virtues, though the Merlot gives a degree of suppleness that is uncharacteristic of a very young Pauillac.

GRAND-PUY-DUCASSE

Successful older vintages appear to include the 1947, 1949, 1953, and 1955. Wines I tasted from the 1970s and early 1980s have been rather light and dilute. Grand-Puy-Ducasse has a genuine Pauillac character, with sweet blackcurrant fruit and cedary tones on the nose, but the wines have been disappointing on the palate, not always well balanced, and sometimes evolving rapidly. It was hard to discern a clear château style, except in negative terms: dilution, occasional greenness, modest length of flavour, a dry finish.

In the vintages from the mid-1980s onwards I detect some improvement: richer fruit, less of the rusticity that marred earlier vintages, and better length. Perhaps the wines continue to lack weight and power, but not every wine from Pauillac needs to compete with Latour or Pichon-Longueville. The 1986 was very good, and the 1988, although still severe and tannic, does have power and richness. I have not tasted the 1989 and 1990 – the latter left Robert Parker distinctly unimpressed – but the 1992 is not bad for the vintage. Both the muscular 1993 and the 1994 show a lack of fruit and elegance but may come together given more time in bottle. Both 1995 and 1996, tasted from cask, were too raw and tannic to judge in their youth.

and spicy, a classic Pauillac, though it seems to be evolving quite fast. The 1991 is very good for the year, though the acidity is quite marked. The 1992 was a success, with ample chunky blackberry fruit and good structure. The 1993 and 1994 were also good for the vintages. The 1995 looks set to become a great Clerc-Milon, and the 1996 looked very promising from cask.

CROIZET-BAGES

Years ago I tasted the 1959; it had a sweet nose, but was drying out on the palate and had little length. The 1961, tasted recently, is similar and lacks distinction. David Peppercorn, a British expert on the wines of Bordeaux, thinks well of the 1962, 1964, 1966, 1971, and 1976. I have tasted the 1979, which was quite sweet and perfumed in its youth; the palate showed firm tannins but little body, and the finish was surprisingly dry. I have not tasted the 1988 and 1989, and the tasting reports of respected colleagues does not encourage me to do so, but the 1990 was mediocre and disap-

GRAND-PUY-LACOSTE

There were great Grand-Puy-Lacoste wines made under Dupin in the 1940s, such as the 1947 and 1949, but the oldest vintage that has come my way is the 1955, which after 40 years was holding up nicely. It was showing tea-like aromas, high acidity without astringency and was decidedly stylish. The estate made impeccable wines in 1961, 1962, and 1966. The 1970 is still packed with very ripe, minty fruit, a most elegant wine, with excellent length of flavour. The 1978 was a rich firm wine, and the following vintage, the 1979, was the first to be made from start to finish by the Bories. It's a fine plump wine, ripe on the nose with a pleasing hint of liquorice; on the palate it is well balanced, lacking some flair, but a classic Pauillac from an underrated year.

The 1982 is first-rate wine. When young it had tremendous attack and length, all of which promised well. Now, approaching maturity, it is evolving beautifully: still dense and concentrated, oaky and succulent, a mouthful of pure pleasure. The 1983 is leaner, but very good. The 1985 and 1986 have excellent reputations, and the 1987 was good for the vintage but should be drunk soon. The 1988 is a brilliant wine: hefty and cedary on the nose, rich, balanced, and concentrated on the palate. It is beginning to reveal both finesse and power. The 1989 is softer and more accessible and will develop more rapidly than the 1988. The 1990 lacks a little complexity, but it's lush, silky, and delicious, with marked new oak aromas. The 1991 is a success for the vintage, but the 1992 is tough and almost medicinal. Both the 1995 and 1996, tasted from cask, are potentially great wines from an estate that has shown remarkable consistency for well over half a century.

HAUT-BAGES-LIBÉRAL

The reputation of this estate is not considered to be especially high. James Seely, writing in 1986 in *Great Bordeaux Wines*, has described its wines as 'uncompromisingly hard', and Hans Walraven believes they lacks depth and intensity. Clive Coates, in *Grands Vins*, has approving if unenthusiastic notes on the 1979, 1982, and 1985. However, the new régime has communicated its commitment to, among others, Robert Parker, who believes there is a case for calling the wine the poor man's Lynch-Bages. The oldest vintage I have tasted is the 1986, which was very good in an old-fashioned way. Very dark in colour, it was closed and almost baked on the nose and dense and thick on the palate – very Pauillac. The 1987 was mediocre, but the 1988, medium-bodied from cask, has put on weight as it has matured. Dark in colour, it has an intense nose of mint and oak, is assertive on the palate, rather closed in terms of fruit expression, but with good length and fine potential. The 1989 is a softer wine, while the 1990 seems more fat and full. The 1993 lacks generosity, and the 1994, while hefty and oaky, seems too chunky and tannic. The 1995 is better, showing more suppleness without any sacrifice of structure or length. The 1996, tasted from cask, had a superb nose, but it's too young to judge.

HAUT-BATAILLEY

After 25 years in bottle, the 1966 was showing mature cedary tones on the nose, but on the palate it remained a bit chunky and lacking in finesse, although it had ample richness and length. Not a great bottle, and a dry finish suggested it was coming towards the end of its life. The 1974 was already cracking up in 1983, perhaps not surprisingly, and the 1975 was not nearly as good as the 1966. There was no undue hardness, as on so many wines of this vintage. Indeed it was quite soft, but lacked concentration and complexity and faded fast on the palate. The 1976 was not bad in the late 1980s, but it too lacked complexity, had baked flavours, and was relatively short; not a bottle to keep. The 1985 is a disappointment. It's a vintage where one might have expected Haut-Batailley to do well, but the wine is

soft, simple, and not especially long. The 1988 is very different: a more tannic, raw, and extracted wine, still showing some bitter-chocolate tones that could become coarse, especially as the finish is dry. The 1989 is as ripe as one would hope for, but the 1990 is disappointing for the vintage and seems to lack weight and complexity, for all its attractive fruitiness and minty finish. The 1994 is well balanced, despite a slight earthiness; there is ample extract and an elegant oaky finish. The 1995 is a more exuberant wine and its spiciness and oak flavours are well integrated. The 1996, tasted from cask, was still too austere to judge.

LYNCH-BAGES

I have not had the privilege to taste very old vintages, but the 1947 and 1949 have a very good reputation. Ten years ago I enjoyed an excellent bottle of 1955, a plump sweetish wine, but not a wine to keep much longer. The 1957 is an old-fashioned Pauillac: tannic

A sampling of Lynch-Bages

and almost severe, which is the character of the vintage, but with good length and a clean finish. The 1959 is said to be superb, and I was very impressed by the 1961: not the most complex of wines, but deliciously fruity, well balanced, and with splendid length of flavour. The 1962 is also a terrific wine with a dense smoky nose and rich compact fruit on the palate. It's a chunky wine and lacks finesse, but it shows remarkable health and vigour given its age.

The 1966 used to be a delicious wine – rich and opulent, soft and mellow, but my notes suggest that it should be drunk soon. The 1970 is one of the great Lynch-Bages, a burly wine of power and solidity. The nose is a cocktail of spice and cherries, the palate surprisingly elegant. The wines of the first half of the 1970s were far from exceptional, though the 1975 is not bad; it has the toughness and dryness of the vintage. The 1978 is good but far from exceptional. The 1979 has a sweet elegant nose, but shows less flair on the palate; it is balanced and well-focused, yet unexciting. Both wines are ready to drink.

In the 1980s two factors seem to have been responsible for a marked improvement in quality: Daniel Llose's winemaking, and the greater use of selection by consigning lesser parcels and lots to the second wine. The 1981 is excellent, a fine wine for a modest vintage. It displays considerably more concentration and vigour than any Lynch-Bages from the late 1970s. The 1982 has been consistently excellent from the earliest days: a rich warm wine with ample tannin and length and new oak flavours. In its youth the 1983 was minty and compact, a wine built to last, but I have not tasted it for many years. The 1985 has all the sweetness and voluptuousness of this delicious vintage. Here Château Lynch-Bages has excelled itself, delivering a wine of tremendous swagger and style, irresistible now but with enough stuffing and extract to keep it alive for many years. I have never encountered the 1986, but other tasters' notes are enthusiastic.

The 1988 has an austerity that is unusual at Lynch-Bages, but that is the character of the year. The wine is still far from ready

Roses and flowering vines in the village of Saint Lambert

and remains dense and chocolatey on the nose and palate. It has tremendous concentration and style and powerful cassis flavours, and after the turn of the century, it will be a fine bottle. The 1989 is sumptuous, showing ultra-ripe fruit, slight cedariness on the palate, and a powerful presence of new oak. This lush wine will give great pleasure for another decade or two, but in terms of elegance it is not quite the match of the superlative 1990, a complex blend of fruit, acidity, and tannin, sumptuous and exuberant. This is surely one of the top Pauillacs of a very great year. It's worth looking out for the 1990 Haut-Bages-Averous, as even the second wine, though lacking the concentration of Lynch-Bages itself, has a delightful cedary aroma, and lush seductive fruit.

Lynch-Bages produced a highly successful wine in 1991; loaded with blackberry and plum fruit, it has remarkable weight and concentration. It is much better and far more structured than the relatively lightweight 1992, an attractive supple wine for drinking over the next few years. The 1993 is a fine effort, showing no unripeness, but I find it hard to warm to its rather lean acidic style, knowing how much fruit and fat Lynch-Bages delivers in a good vintage. The difficulties of the 1994 vintage did not prevent Lynch-Bages from producing an excellent brambly wine, free from harsh tannins, and with good length of flavour. The 1994 Haut-Bages-Averous has a surprising amount of extract for a second wine. Cask tastings of the 1995 and 1996 vintages suggest that both wines will be classic Lynch-Bages: sumptuous, full-flavoured, and packed with supple tannins.

LYNCH-MOUSSAS

Given the run-down and much diminished size of the vineyards until the 1970s, older vintages are rarely encountered. (The French wine writer Bernard Ginestet, however, recalls happy experiences with the 1828 and 1844!) The 1961 is still a wine of considerable vigour and fruitiness, now ready to drink. The vintages of the 1970s were presumably hampered by the abundance of young vines. I have tasted the 1981, which was a pleasant surprise: richly coloured, smoky and minty on the nose, and on the palate concentrated and far from fatigued. Not a great wine, but a fine old-fashioned Pauillac. The problem with Lynch-Moussas in this and other vintages, where high hopes are entertained, is a lack of depth. Take the 1988: a fine cedary, oaky nose, and silky lushness on the palate, but insufficient depth and concentration. Even in 1990 Lynch-Moussas fails to dazzle. There is nothing wrong with the wine; it just doesn't perform as well as it should, given the potential of its vineyards. The 1993 shows the rawness of the vintage; but the 1994 is delicious, ripe and forward, not perhaps a wine for the long haul, but thoroughly enjoyable. The 1996, tasted blind from cask, was impressive in its youth, with power and richness, but the wine was very young and it would be premature to judge it at this stage.

Jalle du Breuil, the stream that separates the communes of Pauillac and Saint Estèphe

PÉDESCLAUX

I tasted the 1983 vintage in 1986 and 1987 and recall how astonishingly forward the wine appeared. The nose was quite jammy, the wine soft, fruity, and without the structure expected in a young Pauillac. However, the 1982 is much better, a well-balanced wine with very attractive fruit; despite its lack of weight and concentration, it is still drinking well. The 1989 is satisfactory, though slightly baked and nutmeggy on the nose; the palate is plump and assertive but the wine has no finesse. Cask samples of the 1995 showed charm rather than richness, and the 1996 was lacking in grip and extraction. Clearly the largely Belgian clientele are satisfied with this wine.

PONTET-CANET

Some of the notes on older vintages that follow should be treated with some caution. I have, thanks to the generosity of Michel Tesseron, tasted many such vintages, but they have all come from the château's cellars. Given the limited château-bottling practiced before 1975, there is likely to be considerable variation among more elderly bottles of Pontet-Canet.

The oldest vintage I have tasted is the cedar-scented 1947, still pungent but showing astringency. It is outclassed by the splendid 1959, which tasted far younger than expected. The wine had blackcurrant and coffee on the nose, high-toned sweet fruit on the palate, and a silky texture and assertive spicy finish – a wine of great vigour

A Pauillac landscape

and remarkable freshness. So is the 1961, though it is more evolved than the 1959, with gamey aromas and a slightly dry finish. It has all the concentration expected from a 1961, and a surprising elegance too. The English-bottled 1964 I bought was, sadly, consumed in 1982, and a charming wine it proved to be, on the light side but with a fine lingering finish.

The 1975 is disappointing, although an English bottling proved slightly better than a château-bottled example, which had evolved rapidly and was lean and sharp on the finish. The 1978, which I have only tasted once, was a curiosity: very deep in colour, yet light in body and hard and tannic on the finish. The 1982 is also disappointing. It shows plenty of sweet attractive fruit, but doesn't have the structure and concentration expected from this great vintage. The 1985 is of greater interest, with a sweet minty nose, and ample plump spicy fruit on the palate. It has recently developed a slight gaminess suggesting the wine is evolving rapidly, but it has good concentration and should keep well.

The 1988 is typical of that vintage: austere, chocolatey, and lacking charm. As it has a powerful tannic grip, concentration and excellent length, it seems probable that it will emerge from its tannic shell in a few years to reveal a powerful, dignified wine, rich in Pauillac typicity. The 1989 is very impressive, although this too is closed and dense, a big tannic wine, highly extracted, still severe. Many 1989s have evolved quite swiftly; not this one, which is built for the long haul. The 1990 seems to get better each time I taste it, as that big chunky fruitiness and chocolatey density begin to knit together. Although extracted and tannic, it is not a tough wine and has the spiciness, power, vigour, and complexity of the best 1990s. A wine with a great future.

Despite the rigorous selection exercised by the Tesserons, I can't derive much pleasure from the 1992, but the 1993 is a considerable success at Pontet-Canet. This is a very deep-coloured wine, with a minty oaky nose. Not exceptionally concentrated, it is supple and elegant and will make a fine bottle for medium-term drinking. The 1994 is delicious, plump and spicy, balanced and stylish. Cask tastings suggest that the 1995 will prove better than the 1996, but time will tell. Certainly the 1995, tasted a few months before bottling, was a delicious blackcurrant wine of fine potential.

LA BÉCASSE

Of recent vintages the 1990 is outstanding, a spicy complex wine of considerable elegance and with supple tannins. Less massive than other 1990s from Pauillac, it is nonetheless a delicious and balanced wine that will age well. In 1992 and 1993 the wine had a higher than usual Merlot component – about 50 percent – and the wines were relatively light. The 1993 is the better of the pair, and is successful considering the difficult vintage.

BELLEGRAVE

The only vintage I have encountered is the excellent 1990: rich and slightly jammy on the nose, with ripe, plump, concentrated flavors, an oaky finish with postive tannins and good length.

BERNADOTTE

The best Bernadotte I have tasted was the 1989, which had a smoky, oaky nose, and ample ripe fruit on the palate and good tannins to keep it lively. The 1993 has a lean, redcurrant nose, but is distinctly light – a pleasant wine for early drinking. The 1995 from cask is very promising: raspberries and menthol on the nose, and plenty of upfront charm rather than power.

CAVE COOPÉRATIVE: LA ROSE PAUILLAC

Among more recent vintages the 1991 lacks structure and length, but is a sound wine from a difficult vintage. I find the 1993 slightly green and acidic. The 1994 and 1995 – ripe, round, supple wines – are much better.

COLOMBIER-MONPELOU

The oldest Colombier-Monpelou I have drunk was the 1975, which was a fairly feeble wine. It was still alive and not overly tannic, but lacked concentration and style. The 1989 is attractive, with a cedary nose, and a palate of well-integrated tannins and a delightful fresh fruit. It is drinking well now, and I see little to be gained by cellaring it further. The 1994 is correct but dull, with blackberry fruit and none of the charm of the 1989. From cask both the 1995 and 1996 struck me as dilute and commercial, pleasant medium-bodied wines for medium-term drinking, with good fruit (especially the 1996) but no elegance or excitement.

CORDEILLAN-BAGES

The estate's first vintage was 1985, a sumptuous wine, ripe and rounded, that could easily be mistaken in a blind tasting for a Napa Valley Cabernet. The 1990 is outstanding, with mint and blackcurrants on the nose, and a fleshy, spicy dimension on the palate. The 1994 is a ripe, succulent, charming wine. It lacks depth but will be an enjoyable bottle for medium-term drinking.

LA FLEUR MILON

The 1964, one of a range of vintages tasted in 1997, had a fine cedary nose of great charm, and a cherry-pie aroma. In flavour the wine is voluptuous and far from tiring. The 1971 was disappointing, very mature, and was drying out and dour on the palate. The 1982 is splendid: deep in colour, though showing some maturity. On the palate it is rich and concentrated, entirely Pauillac in its vigour, structure and spectrum of flavours.

The 1986 is a softer and more elegant wine than I would have expected from this vintage; its strong vanilla tones are surprising in a wine that has seen no new oak. The 1991 is a success for the vintage, cedary and robust on the nose, full-flavoured and long on the palate. I find the 1993 dour, and slightly herbaceous, but the 1994 is very good, in a chunky, lush style. The 1995 is more concentrated and extracted. A cask sample of the 1996 was also impressive.

LA FLEUR PEYRABON

The 1990 is simply delicious, a stylish wine with lovely fruit and plenty of backbone. The 1991 is well balanced, a charming delicate wine that is not overextracted. The 1992 has the deficiencies of the vintage: simplicity, dilution, and some astringency. The 1993 is little better: green and rather short. The 1995 shows the tremendous ripeness of the year, and a bracing oakiness – a very good wine, but if only it had more concentration!

FONBADET

I have not had the opportunity to taste old vintages of Fonbadet. The 1982 is said to be excellent. I found the 1990 an enticing wine, ripe and elegant on the nose, with a minty intensity and opulence. It has real Pauillac typicity and exceptional length of flavour. It is a powerful wine that is approachable young but will keep well. The 1995, tasted from cask, is also rich and concentrated, with fine balance and length. It should develop nicely with time.

HAUT-LINAGE

I have only tasted the wine from cask, so it is difficult to make a firm judgement as to its quality. I had the impression that Haut-Linage is medium-bodied, quite fruity, and clean, despite the rusticity of the winemaking, but there is a lack of concentration.

PIBRAN

Both the 1989 and 1990 are delicious wines. The 1989 has a milk-chocolate nose (which is more positive than it sounds), and is plump and silky on the palate, lightly structured but well balanced. The 1990 is similar, but more complex on the nose, with notes of coffee and mint. On the palate it is rich, succulent, and generous. Both are drinking well in the late 1990s but could be kept.

The 1992 is not bad for the vintage. It is firm but not over-extracted. It is overshadowed by the more opulent 1994, with its lush blackberry fruit and svelte texture. The 1995 lacks depth for all its overt fruitiness; this may be a consequence of young vines.

PLANTEY

The vintages I have tasted – 1988, 1994, and 1995 – have a similar character: a fresh raspberry and cherry fruitiness on the nose, and on the palate a medium-bodied juiciness that is a touch cloying. The wine cries out for the moderating complexity of oak-ageing.

SAINT MAMBERT

The 1993 shows too much oak for the fruit, but the 1994 is rich and spicy, with plenty of extract – a solid, well-balanced wine with undeniable Pauillac typicity. The more overtly fruity 1995 has less typicity, at least from cask, but is a wine of considerable charm.

LA TOURETTE

Given the immense care Larose-Trintaudon take over this wine, I find the results slightly disappointing. In its youth the 1993 was raw and astringent, but it may well soften in time. The 1994 is better, very oaky on the nose, a soft plump wine of fair concentration. The 1995, predictably, is much better, though the new oak on the nose initially obscures the fruit. But the wine is rich and spicy, and the tannins bode well for its development in bottle.

LA TOUR PIBRAN

The 1990 is a fruity, attractive wine, not complex, but savoury and enjoyable. The 1992 was a difficult vintage, and La Tour Pibran produced a wine that is rather dilute, although it has some charm and richness. The 1993 shows a slight bitterness on the finish that may vanish with bottle age.

Carpenter's shop in the village of Saint Lambert

Bibliography

D'Armailhacq, Armand. *La Culture des Vignes dans le Médoc*. Second edition. Bordeaux, 1858.

Bourdet, Denise. *Lafite Rothschild*. Paris, 1990.

Coates, Clive. *Grand Vin*. London: Weidenfeld & Nicolson, 1995.

Dethier, Jean, ed. *Châteaux Bordeaux*. London: Mitchell Beazley, 1989.

Faith, Nicholas. *Latour*. London: Christie's, 1991.

Féret, Claude. *Bordeaux and Its Wines*. Thirteenth edition. Bordeaux: Féret, 1986.

Ginestet, Bernard. *Pauillac*. Paris: Legrand, 1985.

Higounet, Charles. *La Seigneurie et le Vignoble de Château Latour*. Bordeaux: Fédération Historique du Sud-Ouest, 1974.

Parker, Robert M., Jr. *Bordeaux*. Second edition. New York: Simon & Schuster, 1985.

Penning-Rowsell, Edmund. *The Wines of Bordeaux*. London: Penguin, 1976.

Peppercorn, David. *Bordeaux*. Second edition. London: Faber, 1991.

Pijassou, René. *Le Médoc*. Paris: Tallandier, 1980.

Ray, Cyril. *Lafite*. Third edition. London: Christie's, 1985.

Seely, James. *Great Bordeaux Wines*. London: Secker & Warburg, 1986.

The courtyard of Château Batailley

Index

Acknowledgements

Many people in London and the Bordeaux region have helped me as I researched this book, and I particularly wish to thank Gerald Asher, François-Xavier Borie, Émile Castéja, André Cazes, Jean-Michel Cazes, Charles Chevallier, Nicholas Faith, Daniel Llose, Fiona Morrison MW, Sylvie Cazes-Régimbeau, Caroline Dedieu, May-Eliane de Lencquesaing, Pierre and Pascale Peyronie, Jancis Robinson MW, Christian Le Sommer, Alfred Tesseron, Claire Villars-Lurton, Jean-Louis Viaut and Elodie Suhas of the Conseil des Vins du Médoc, and Jean-Marc Guiraud of the Union des Grands Crus de Bordeaux.

I would like to express special thanks to Michel and Diane Tesseron, who gave me the free run of Château Lafon-Rochet while I was in the Médoc, thus offering me the opportunity to work and rest in the most comfortable and tranquil environment imaginable.

Thanks must also go to Margaret Little, Fiona Knowles, and Jane Aspden of Mitchell Beazley, who provided many valuable suggestions during the course of this project.

I am also most grateful to John Tucker of Norfleet Press, New York, who initiated this project and kept a close eye on its evolution from manuscript to finished book. He was generously assisted by Abby Goldstein, Patricia Wyatt, Eunice Fried, William Jelenko, Marie Mangeot, James Owen Mathews, Gina Webster, and Carmen Young.   S.B.

A walk through Pauillac